Maze Art Book

By Stacie Ann Leininger

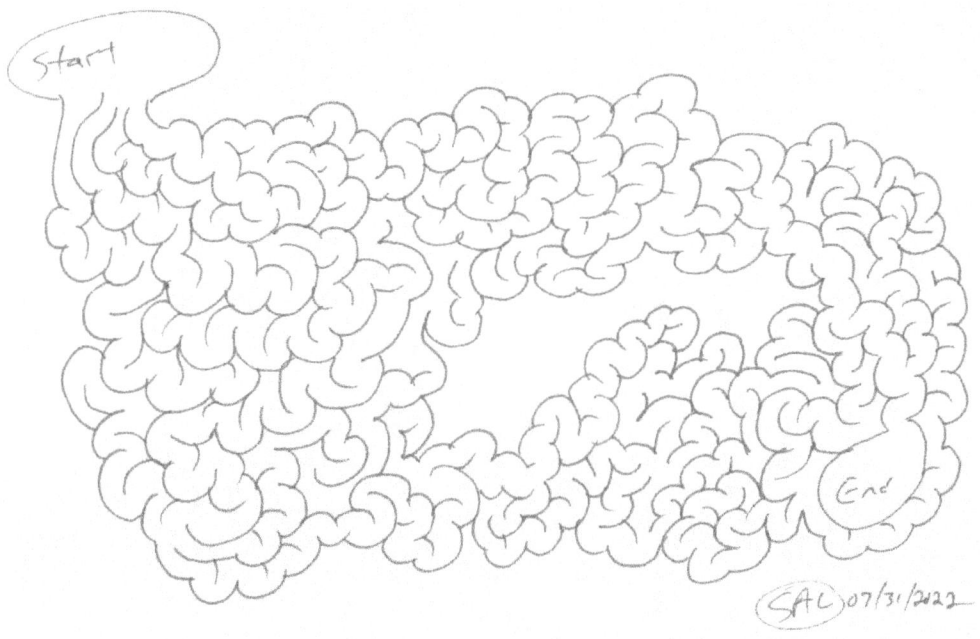

Mazes are all created by using pen on paper, then scanned in for digital cleanup. A couple of these mazes have had minimal cleanup done to keep their original artistic rustic feel.

Gleothane, Inc.

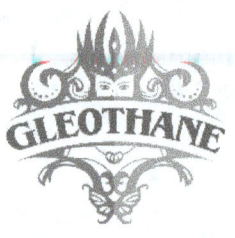

ISBN:

Cover design by: Stacie Ann Leininger
Printed in the United States of America

DEDICATION

To Andrea Walton 1980-2020
the fearless friend who encouraged me to fight when others pushed me to back down.

ACKNOWLEDGMENTS

I started making mazes at a young age as a competition between my older brother and myself. In 5th grade, a classmate saw me practicing on making a difficult maze and asked to try it.

Then in Junior high Andrea Walton asked me why I wasn't making photocopies and selling those instead of giving away originals.

From 1992 to 1998 Andrea encouraged me to make my mazes more difficult and remained my go to person for the sales of my mazes.

In memory of Andrea and her encouragement, I have not included answer keys as she was adamant the best part of my mazes was figuring out the solution on her own.

Mazes in this book range in difficulties and stand alone as art by themselves. Each of my mazes are drawn on paper with a pen, then scanned in to be cleaned up for my maze art books. A couple of the mazes, in this book, have had minimal cleanup to keep their rustic artistic feel.

It is also important that I acknowledge my unnamed 5th grade classmate for being my best repeat customer all the way to High School graduation.

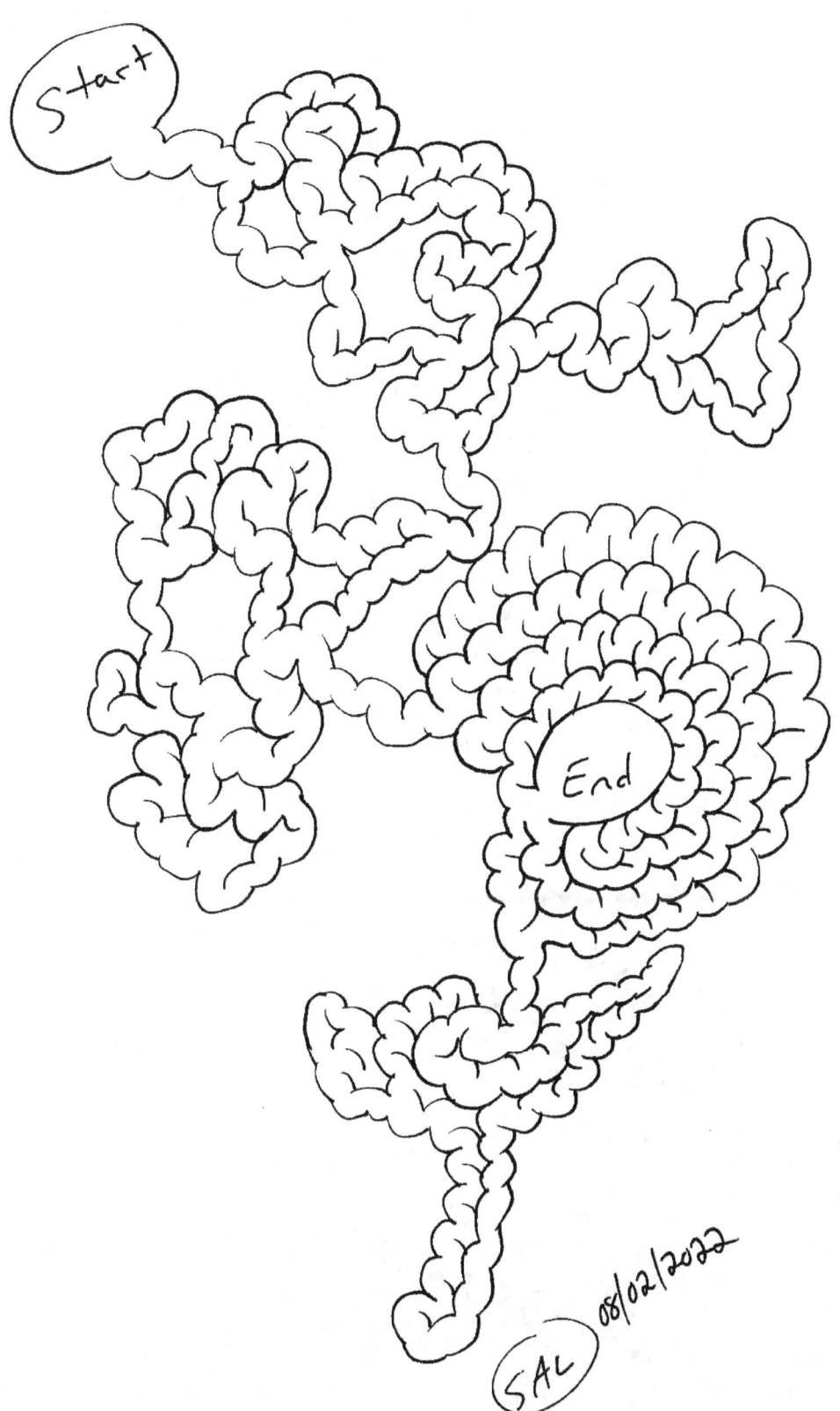

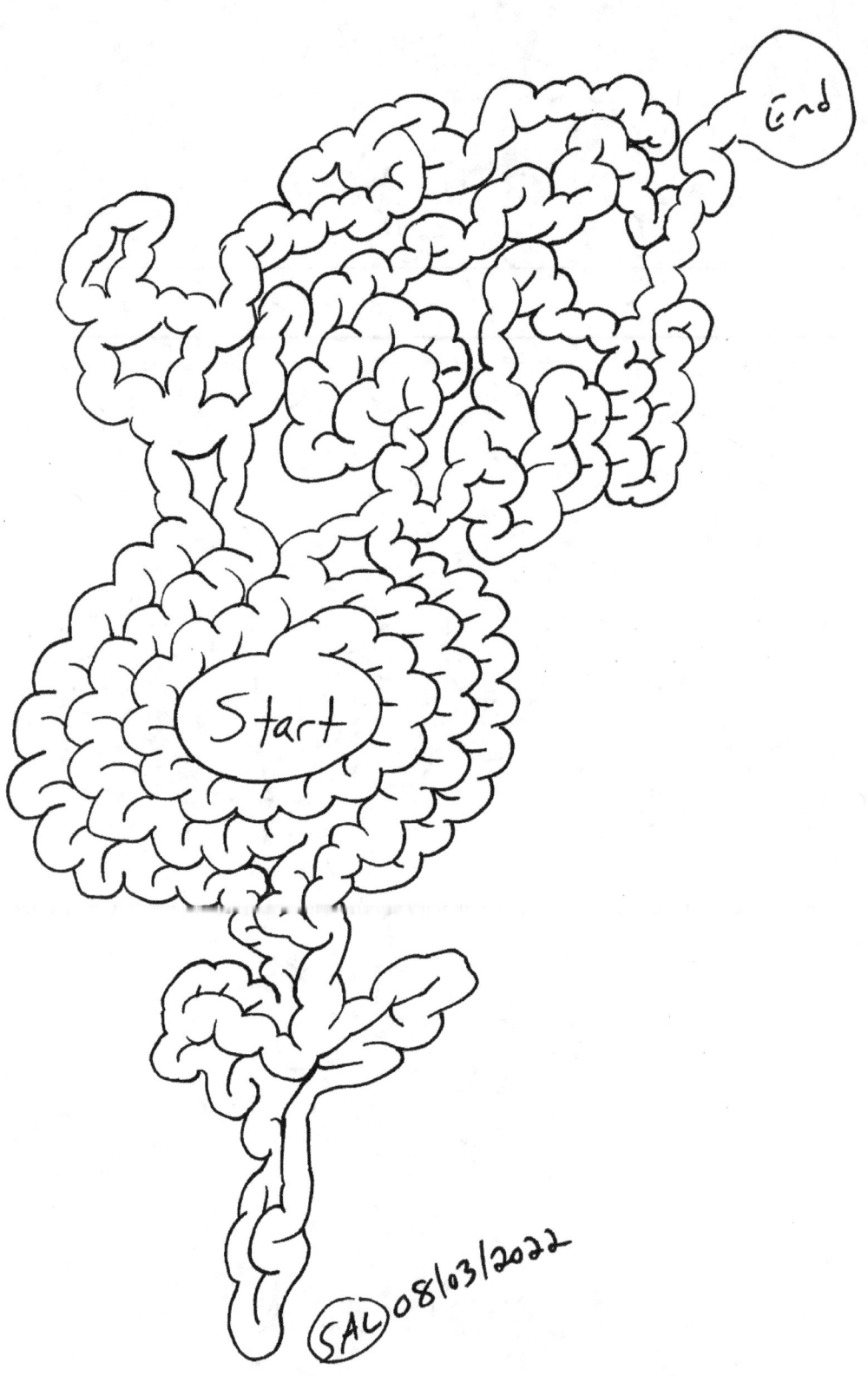

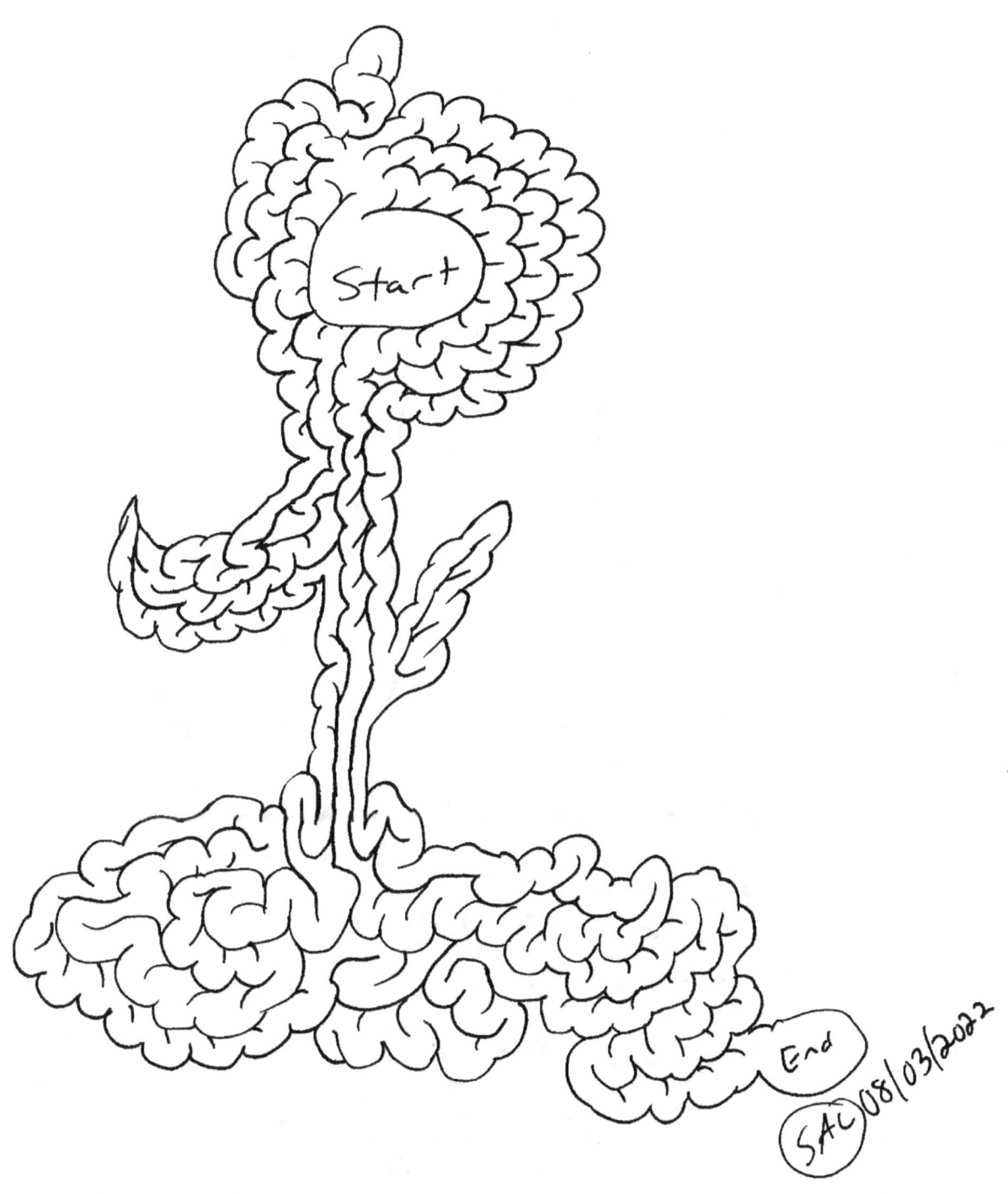

Start

End

SAC 08/03/2022

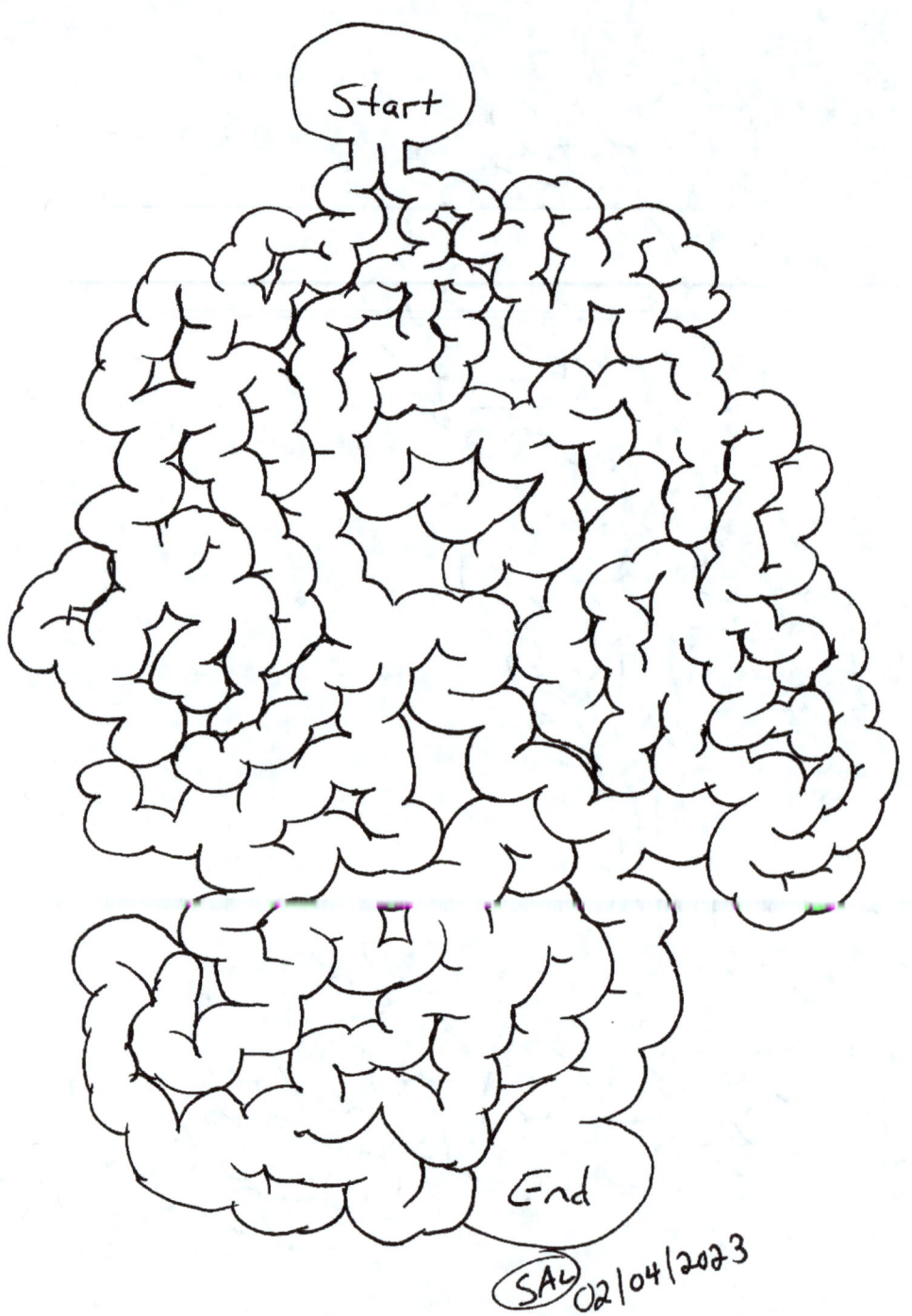

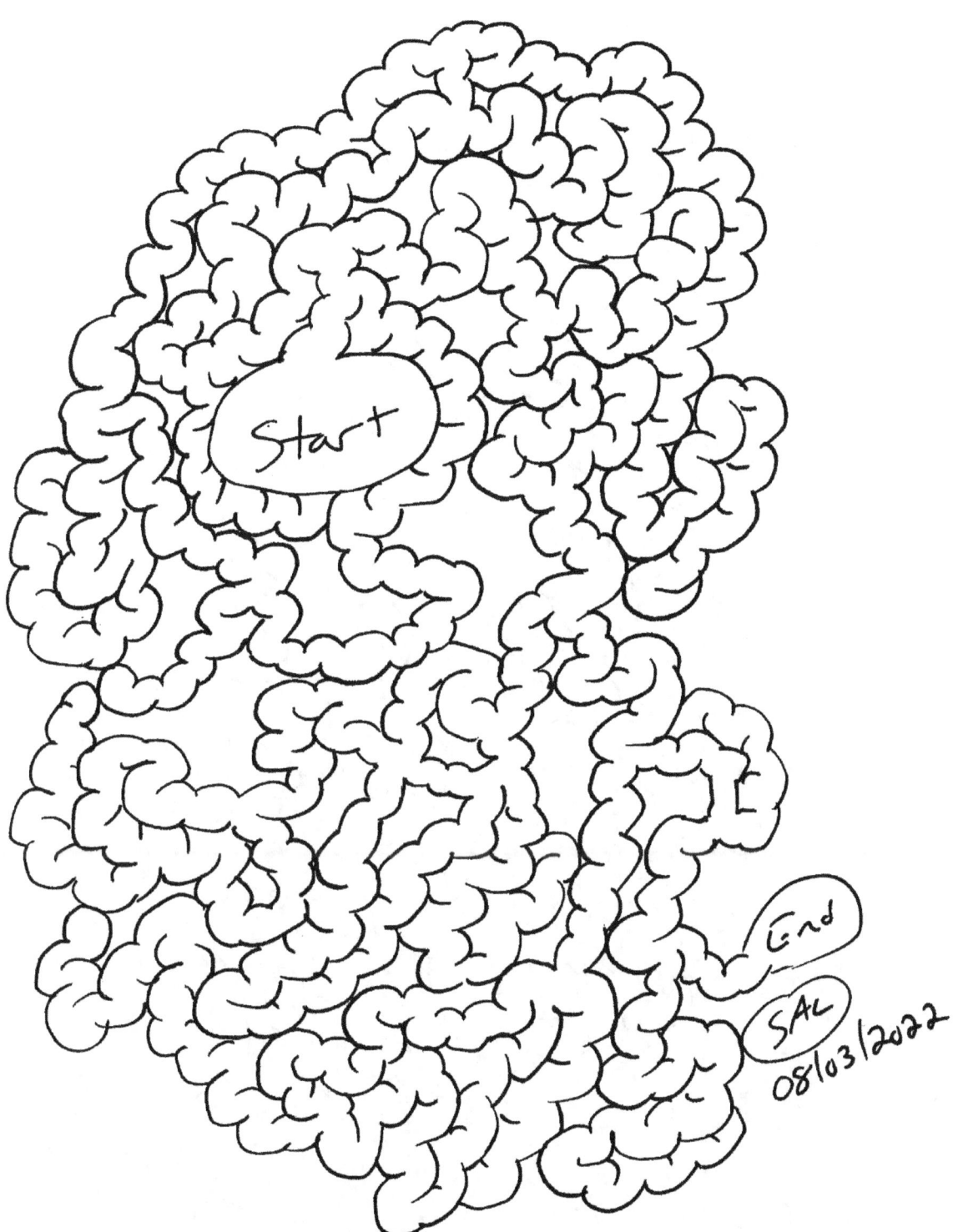

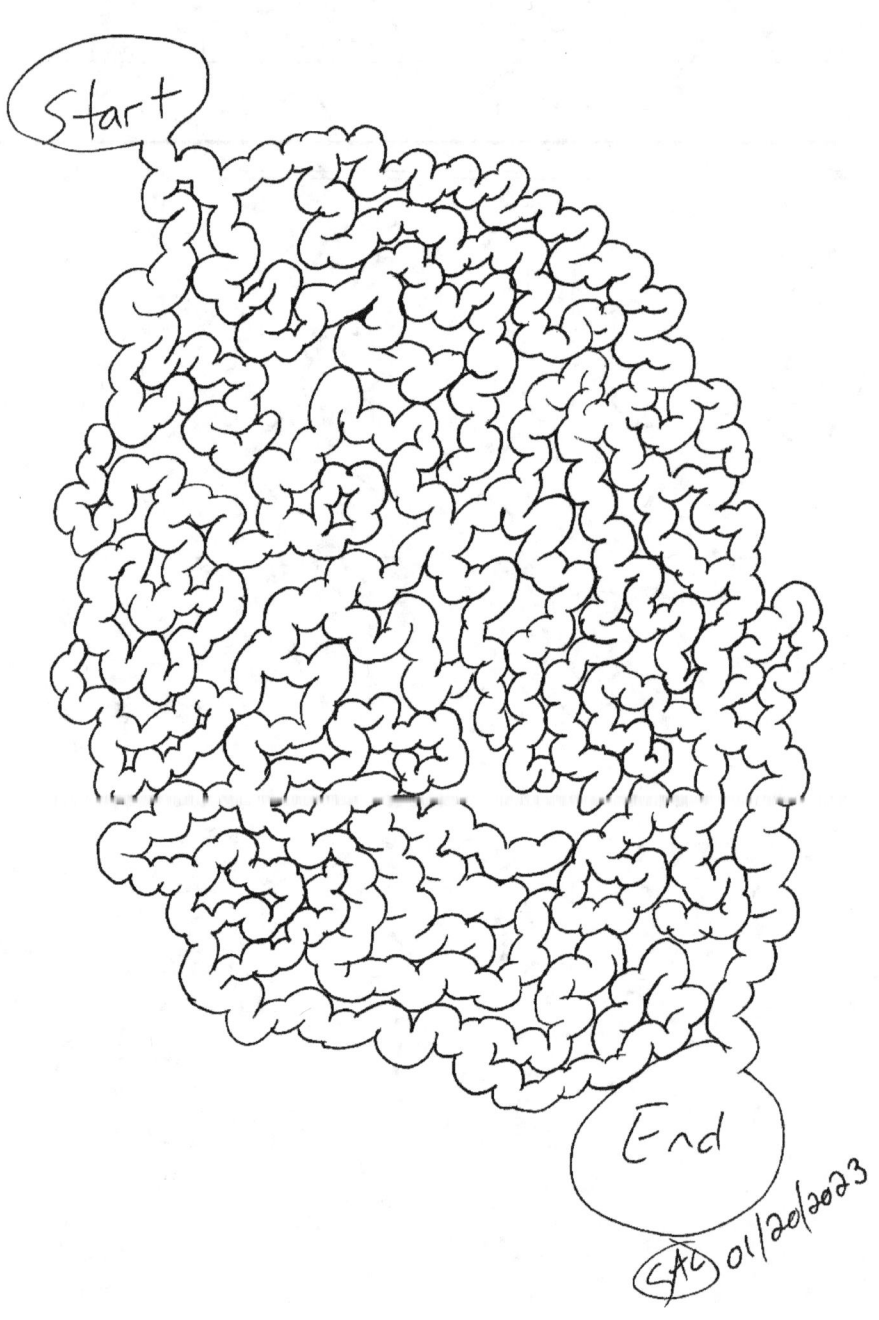

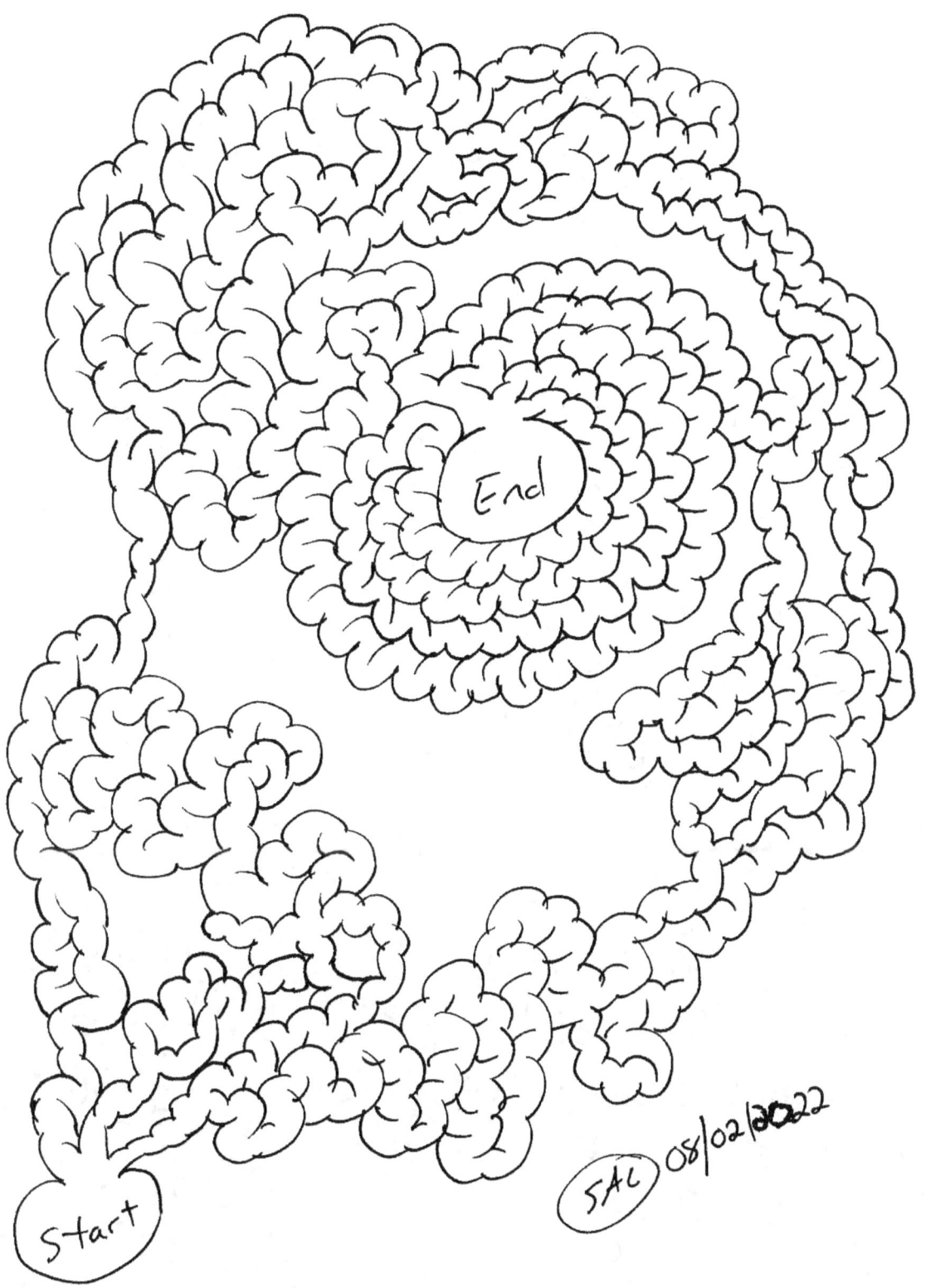

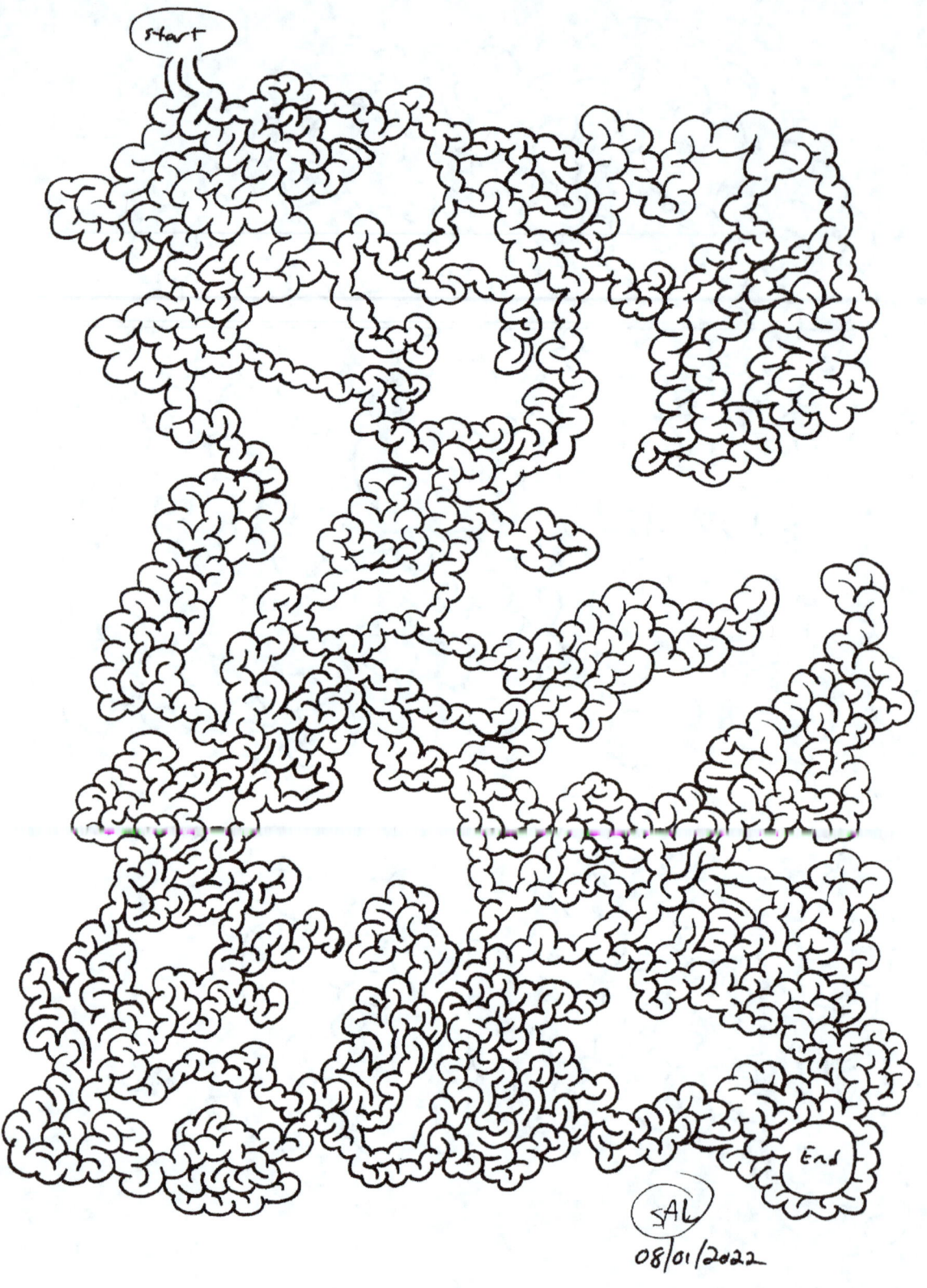

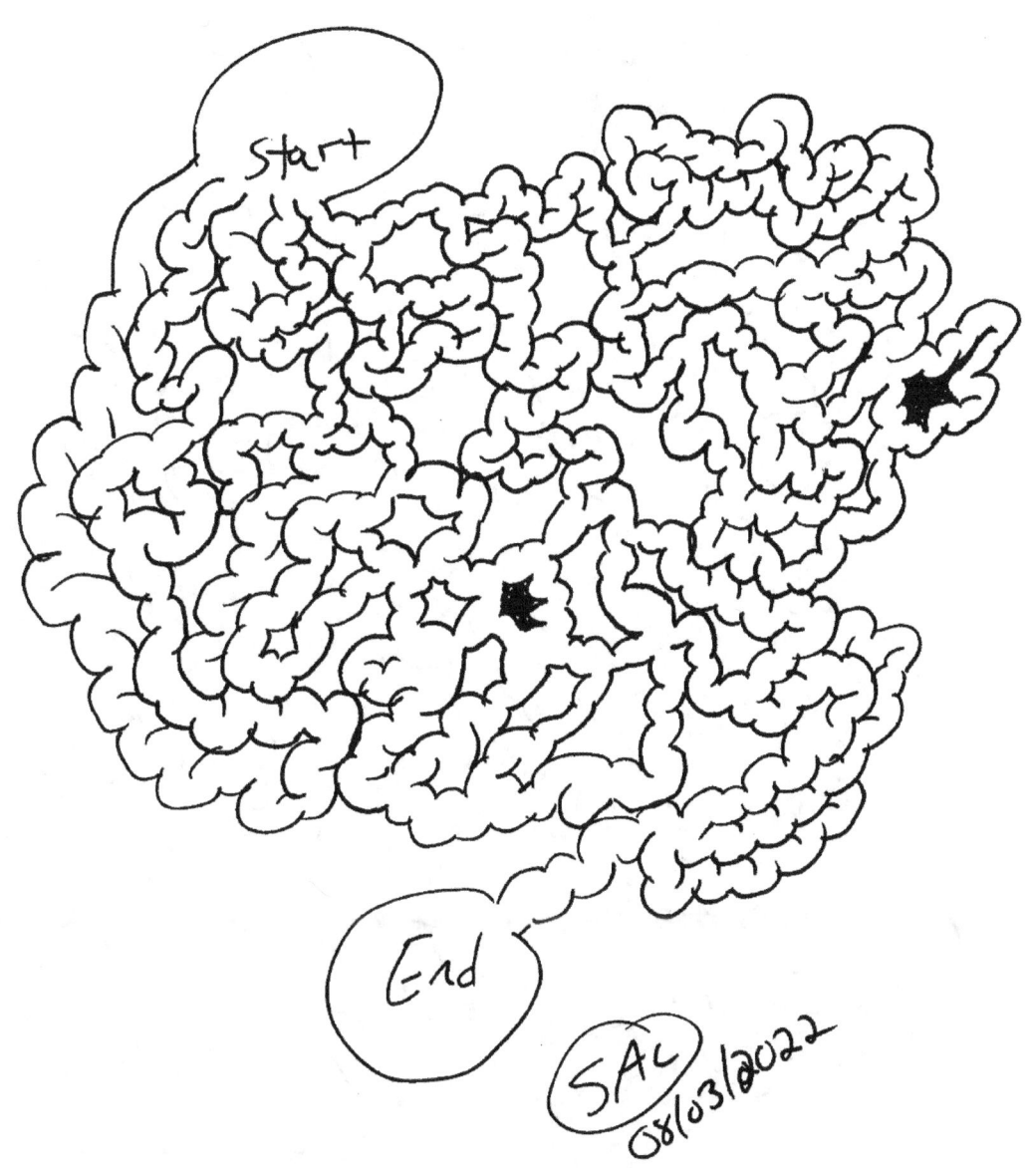

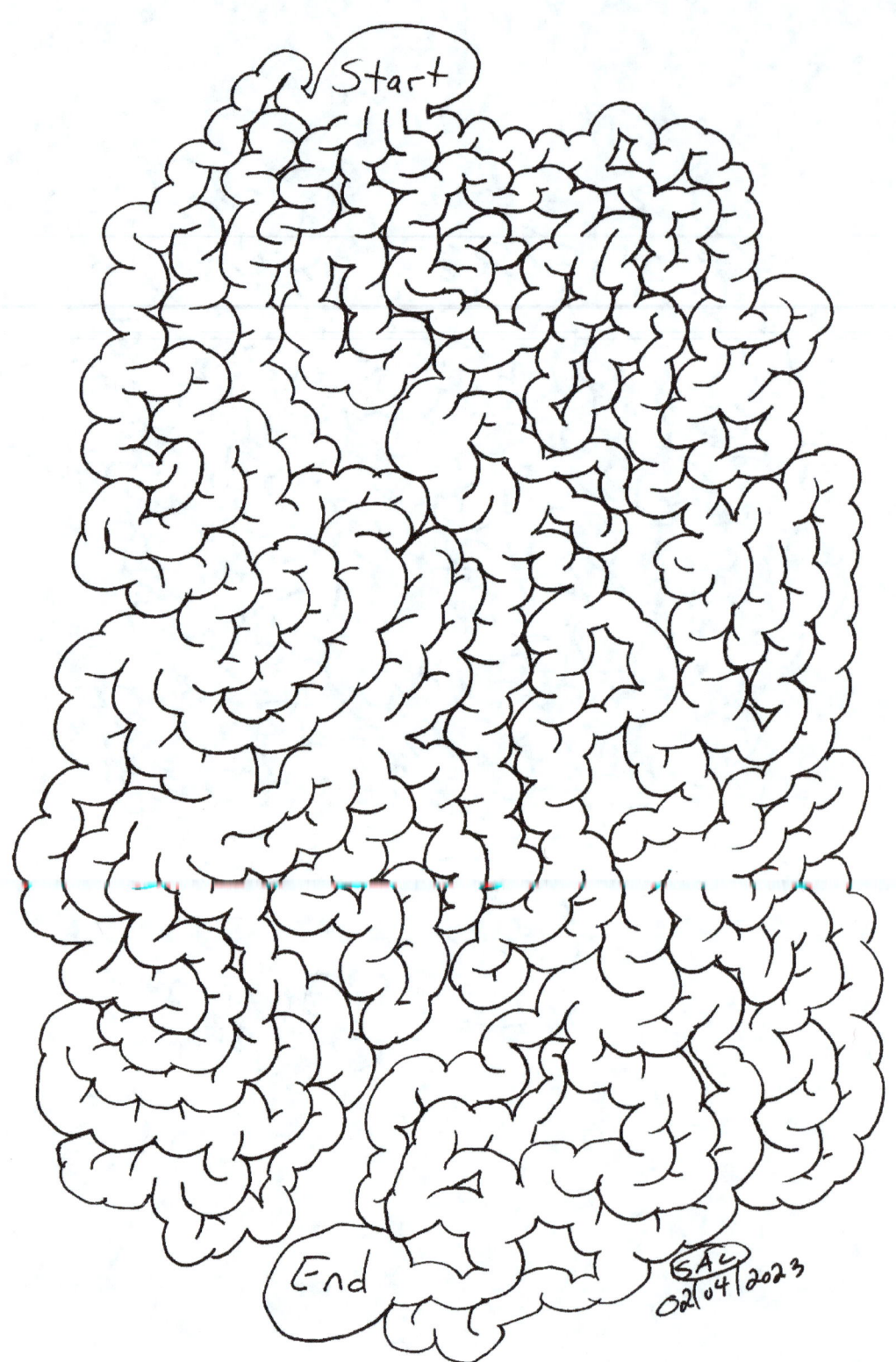

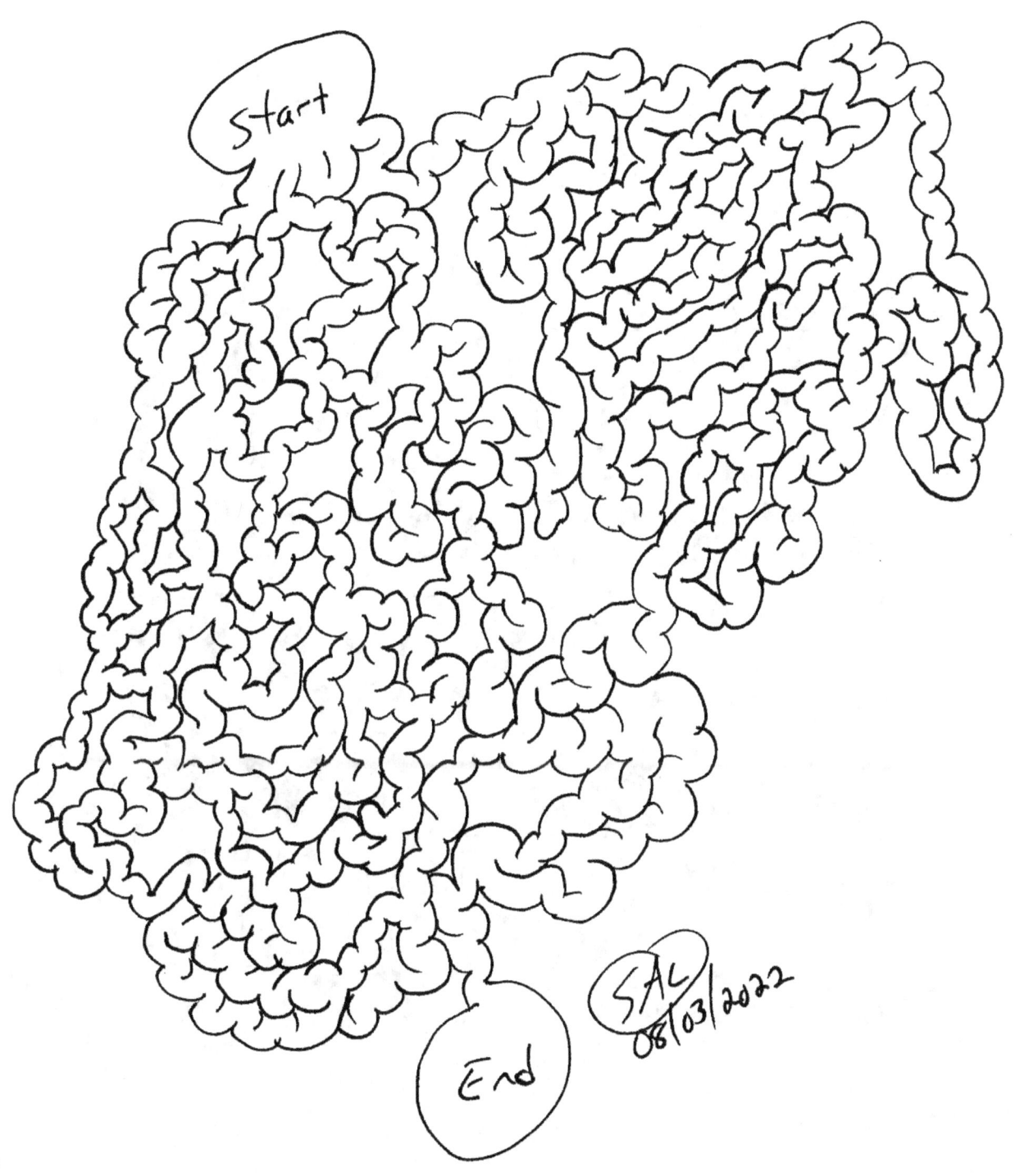

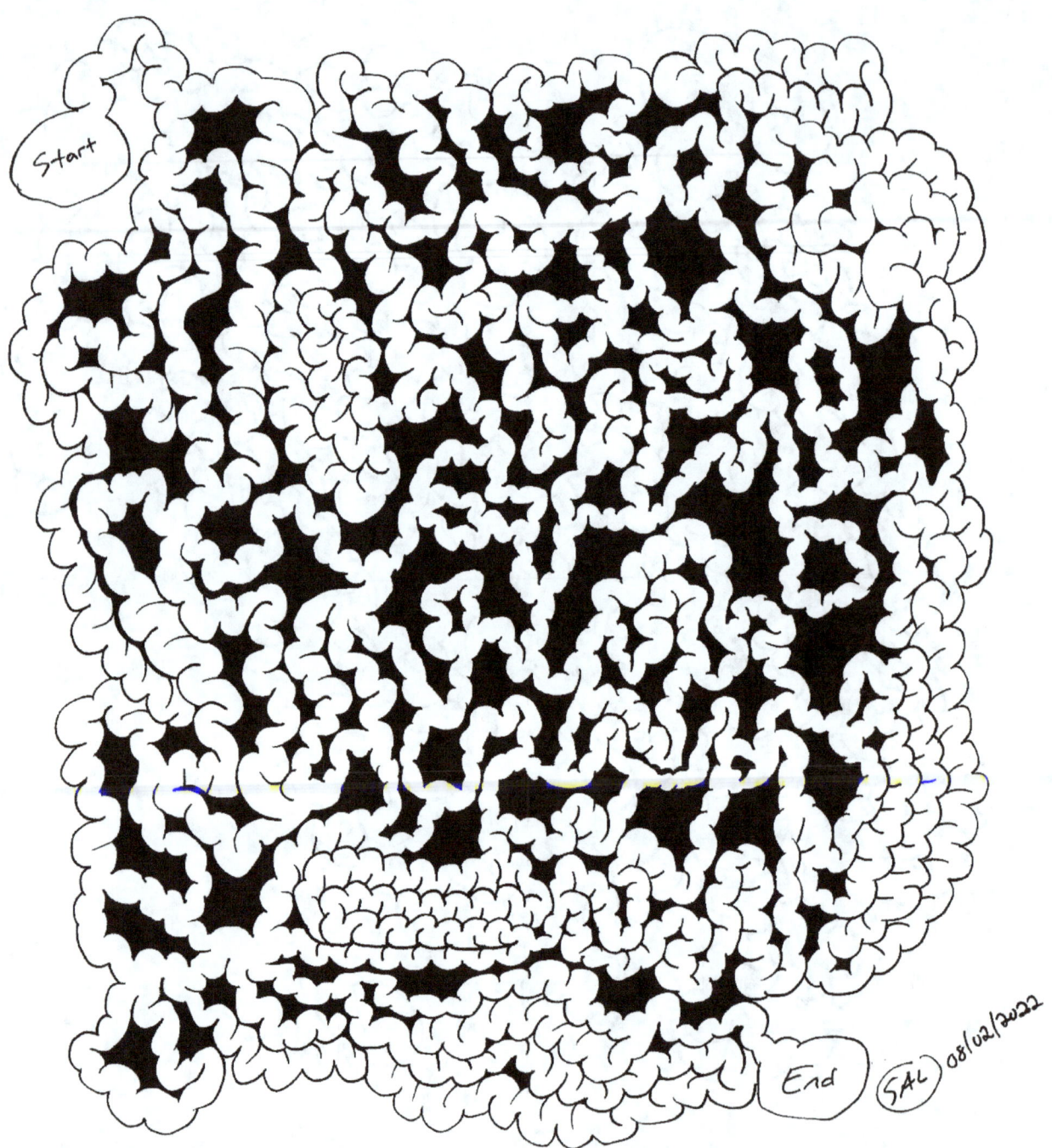

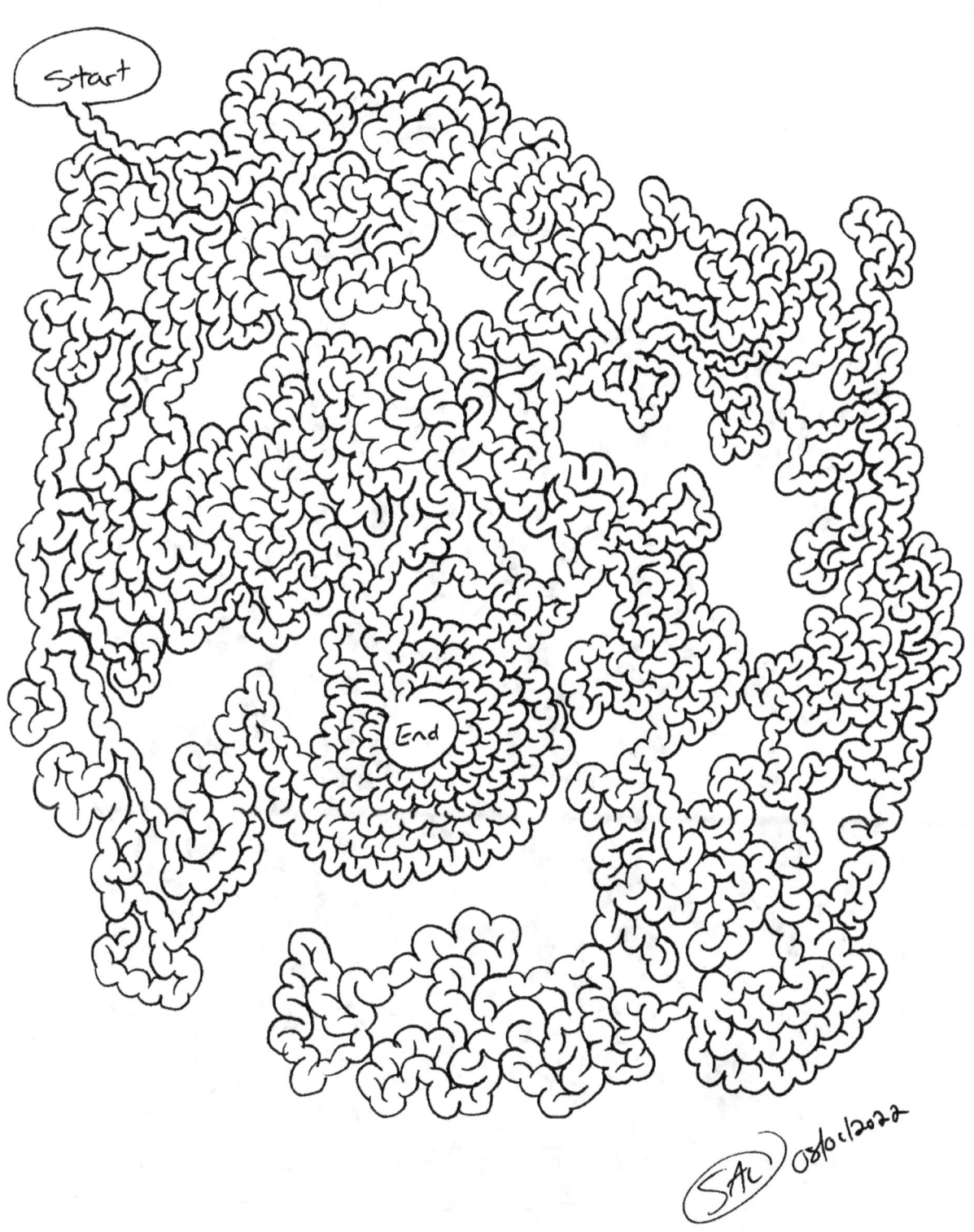

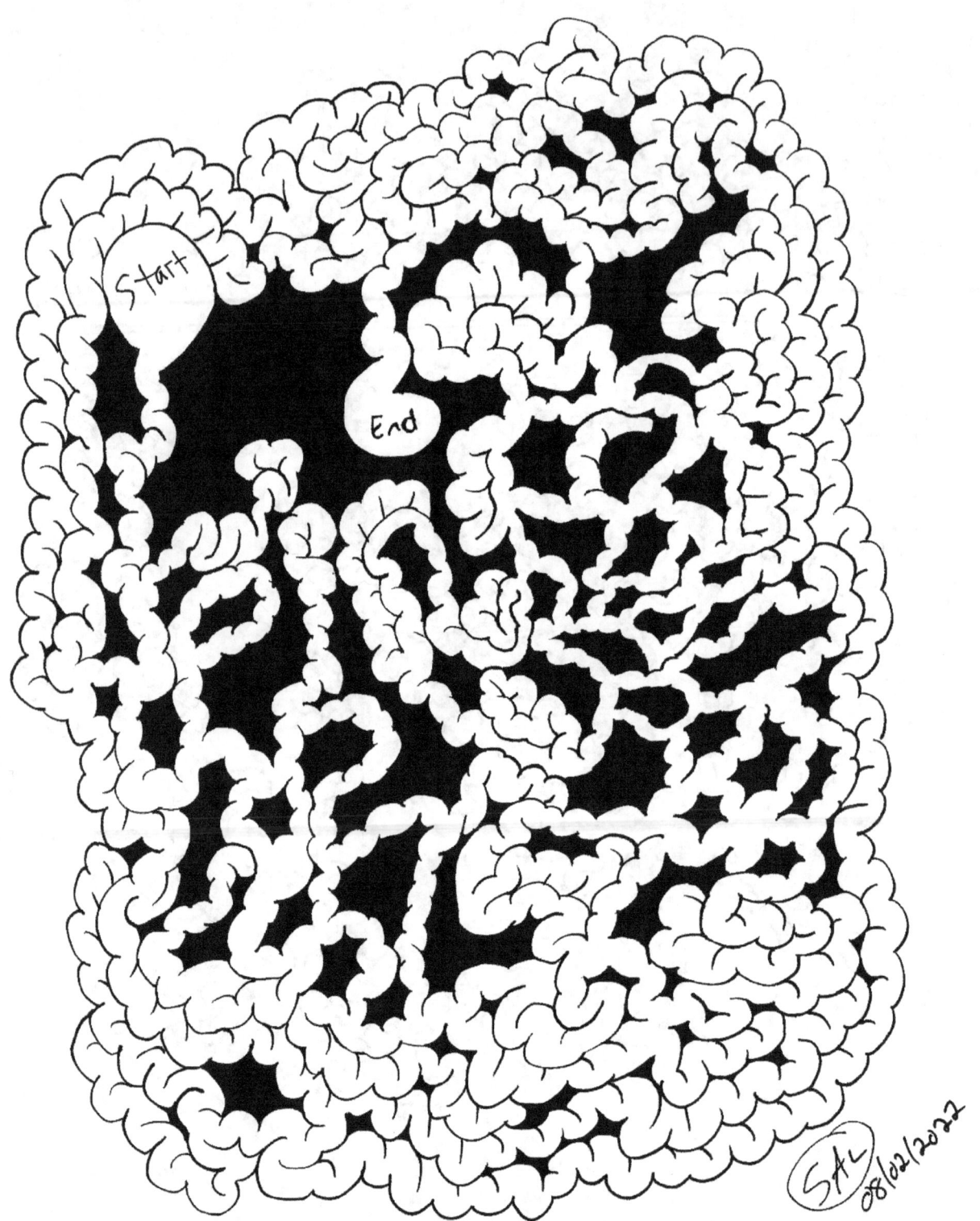

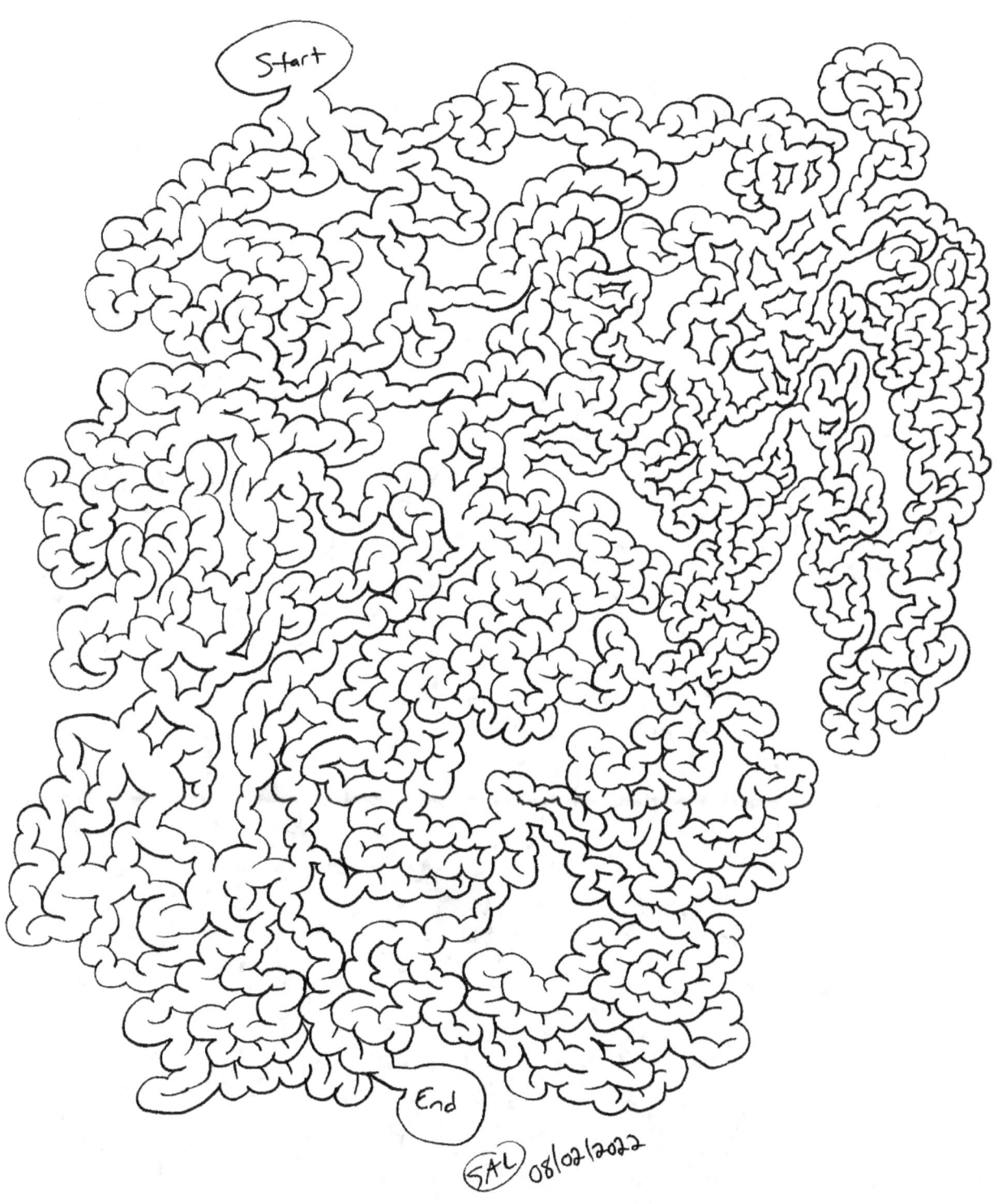

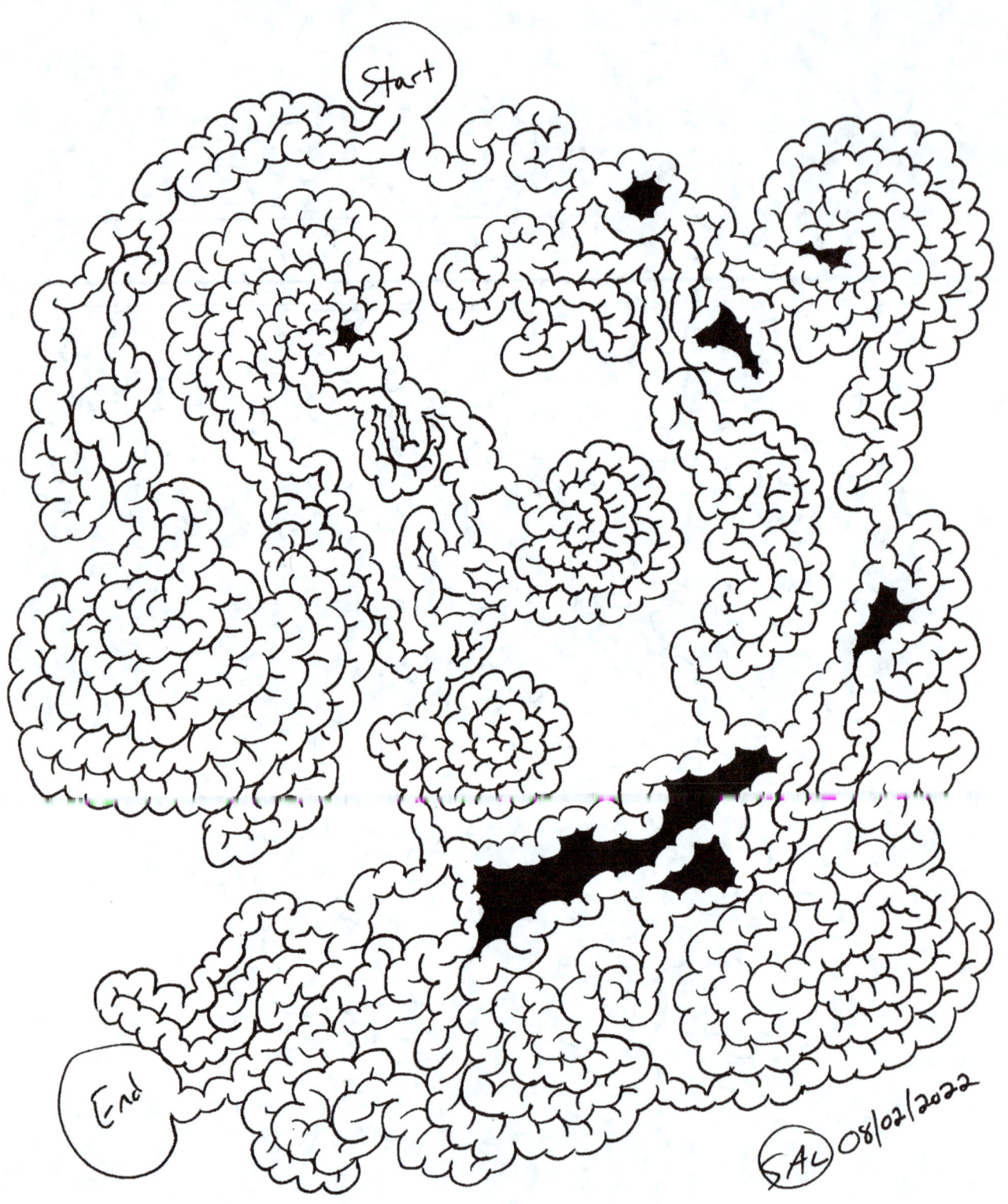

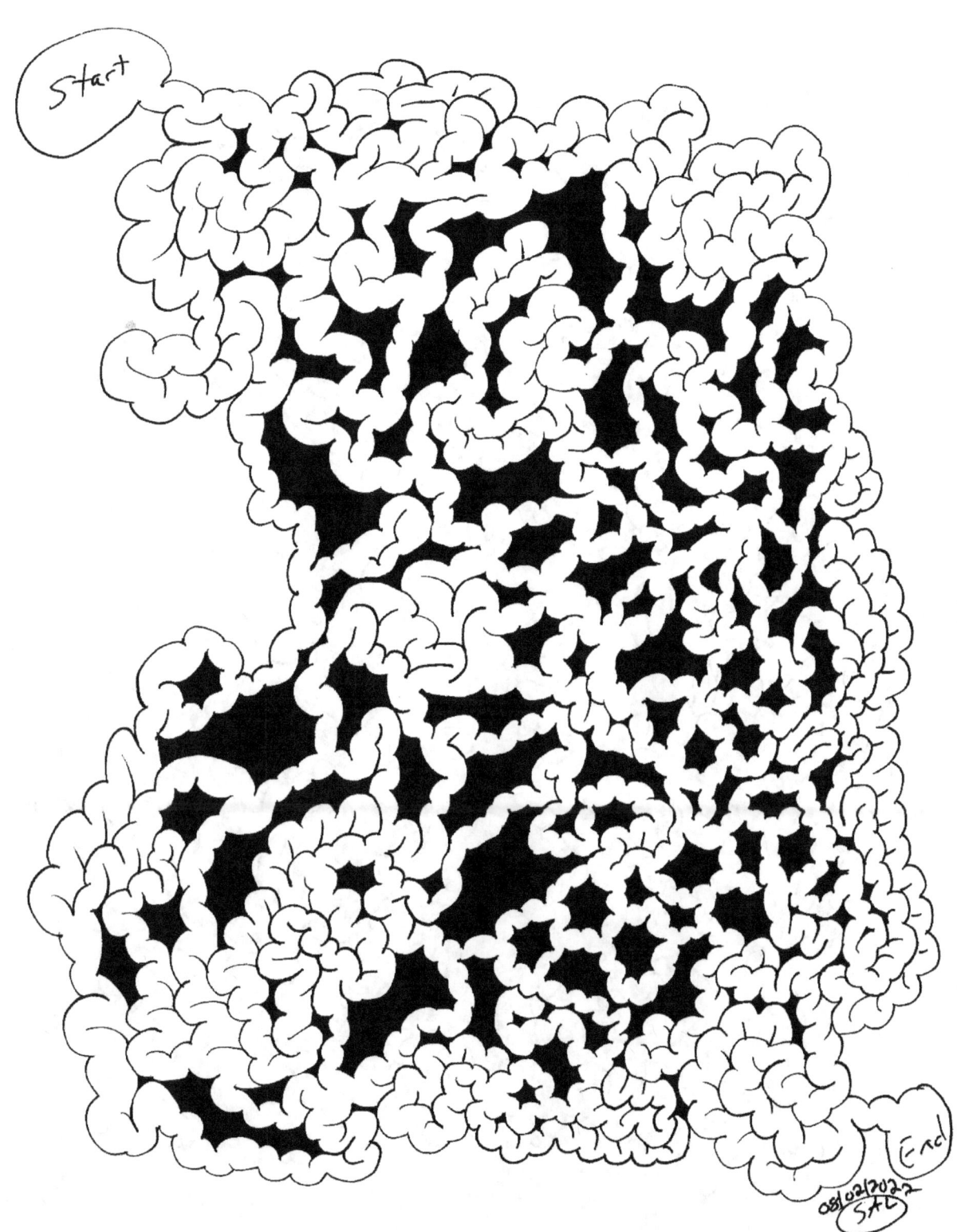

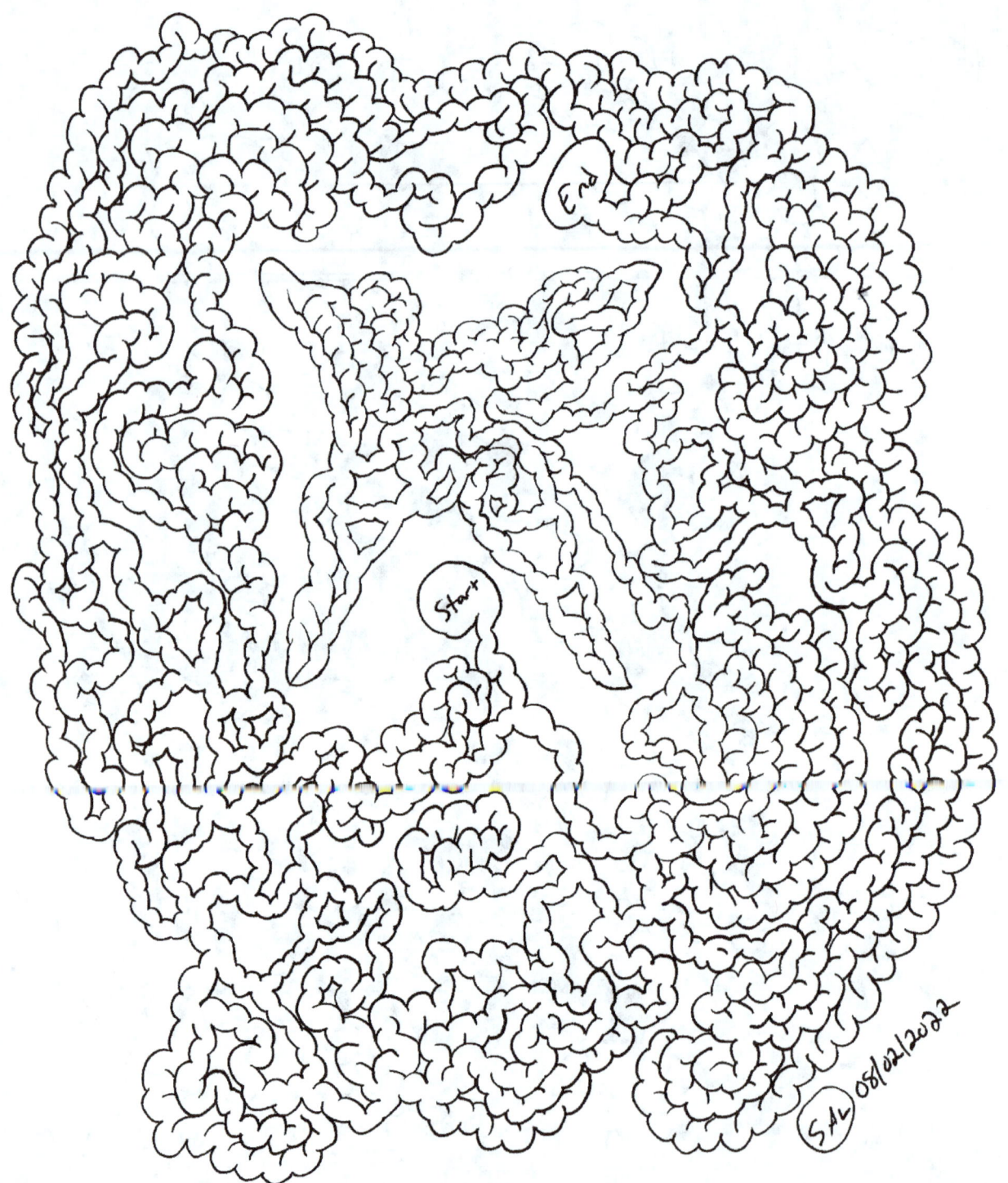

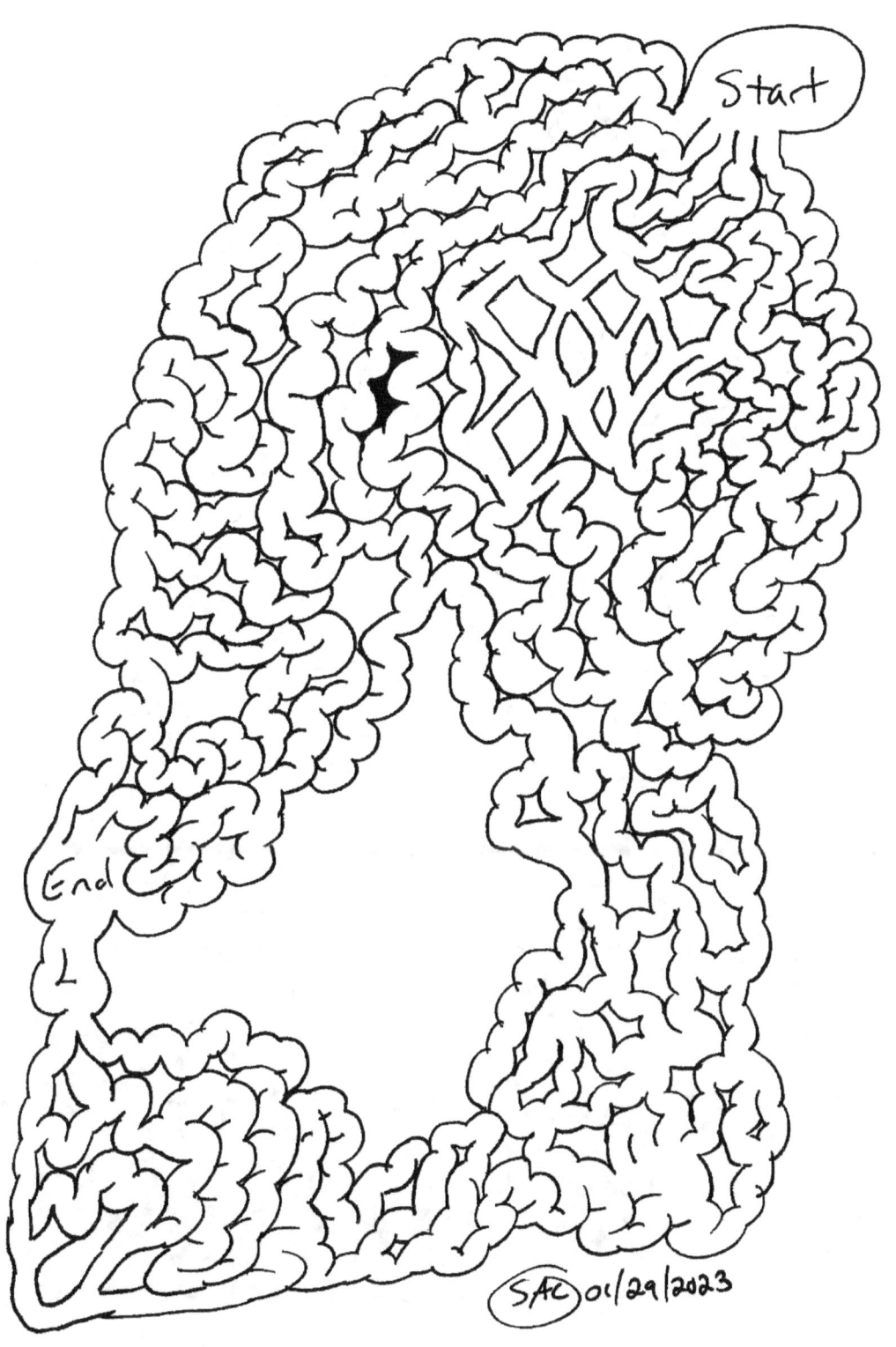

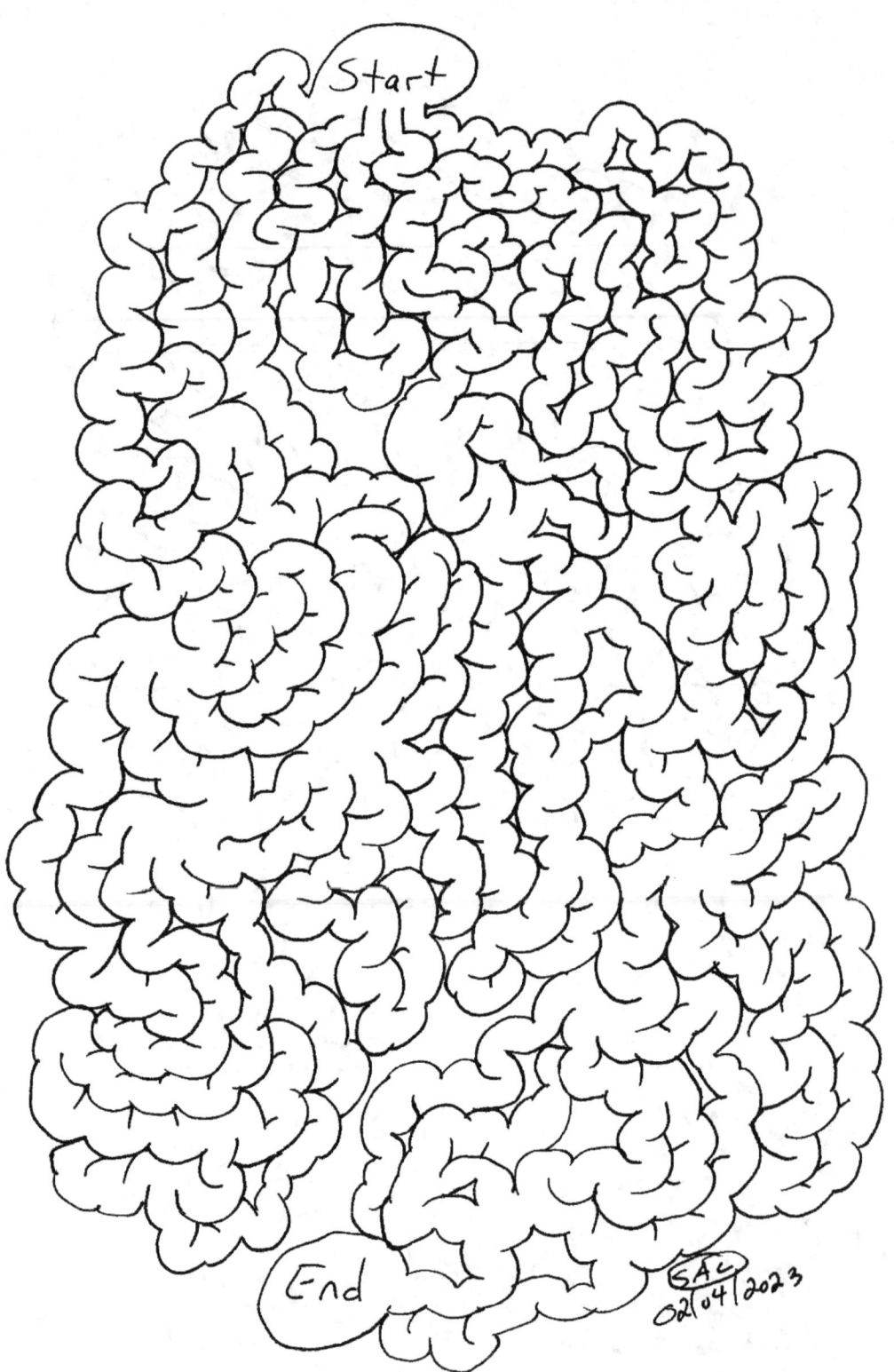

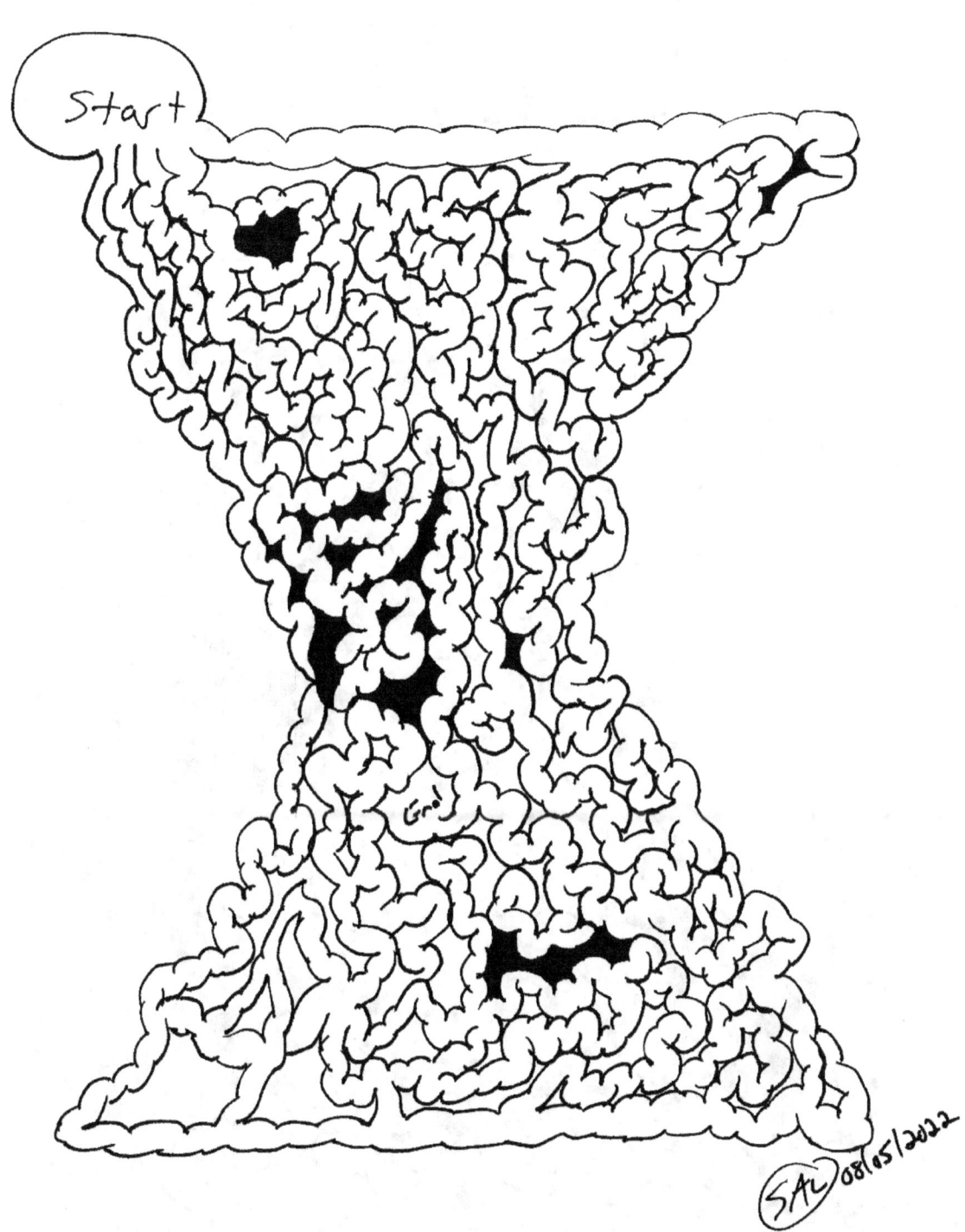

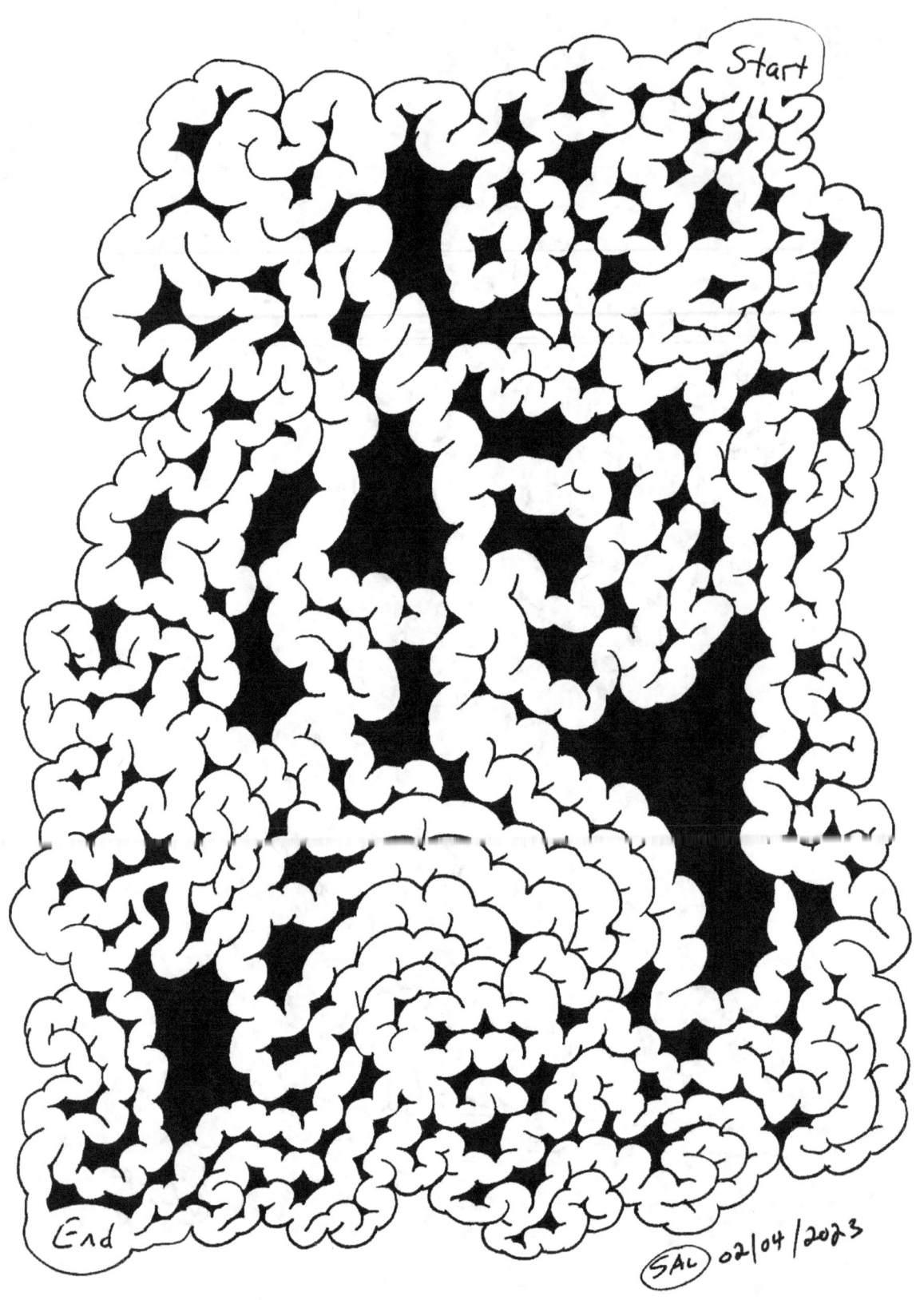

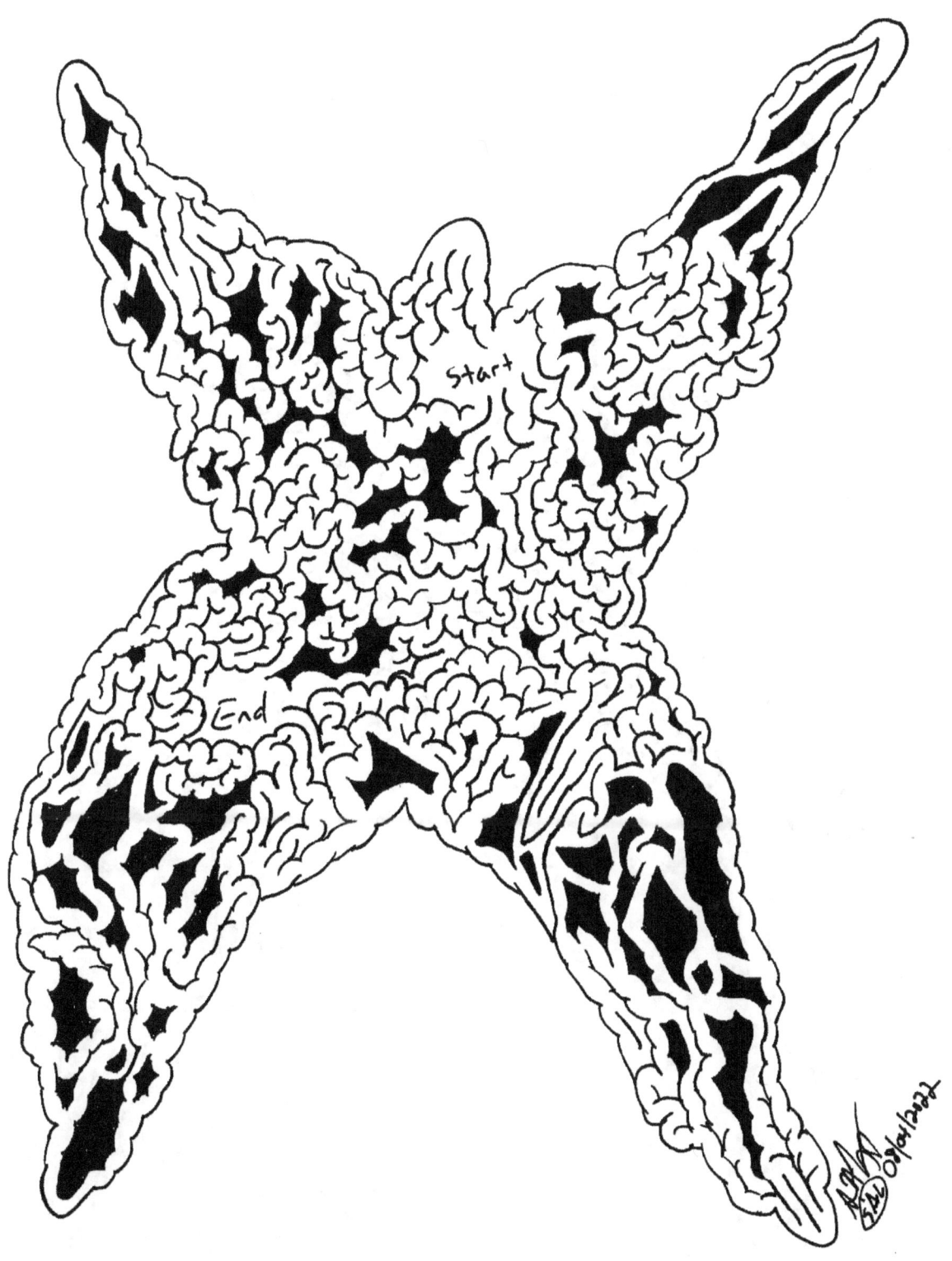

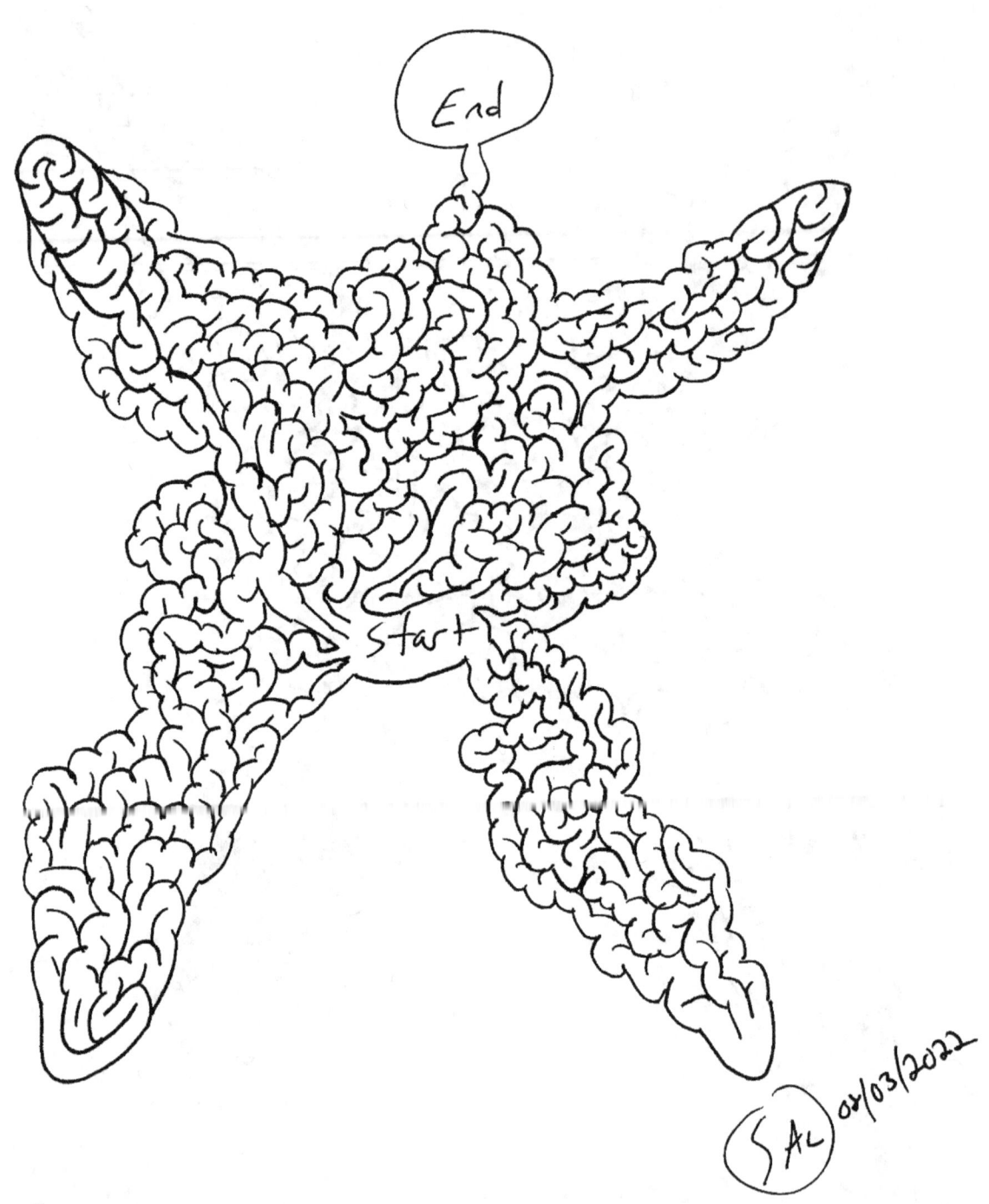

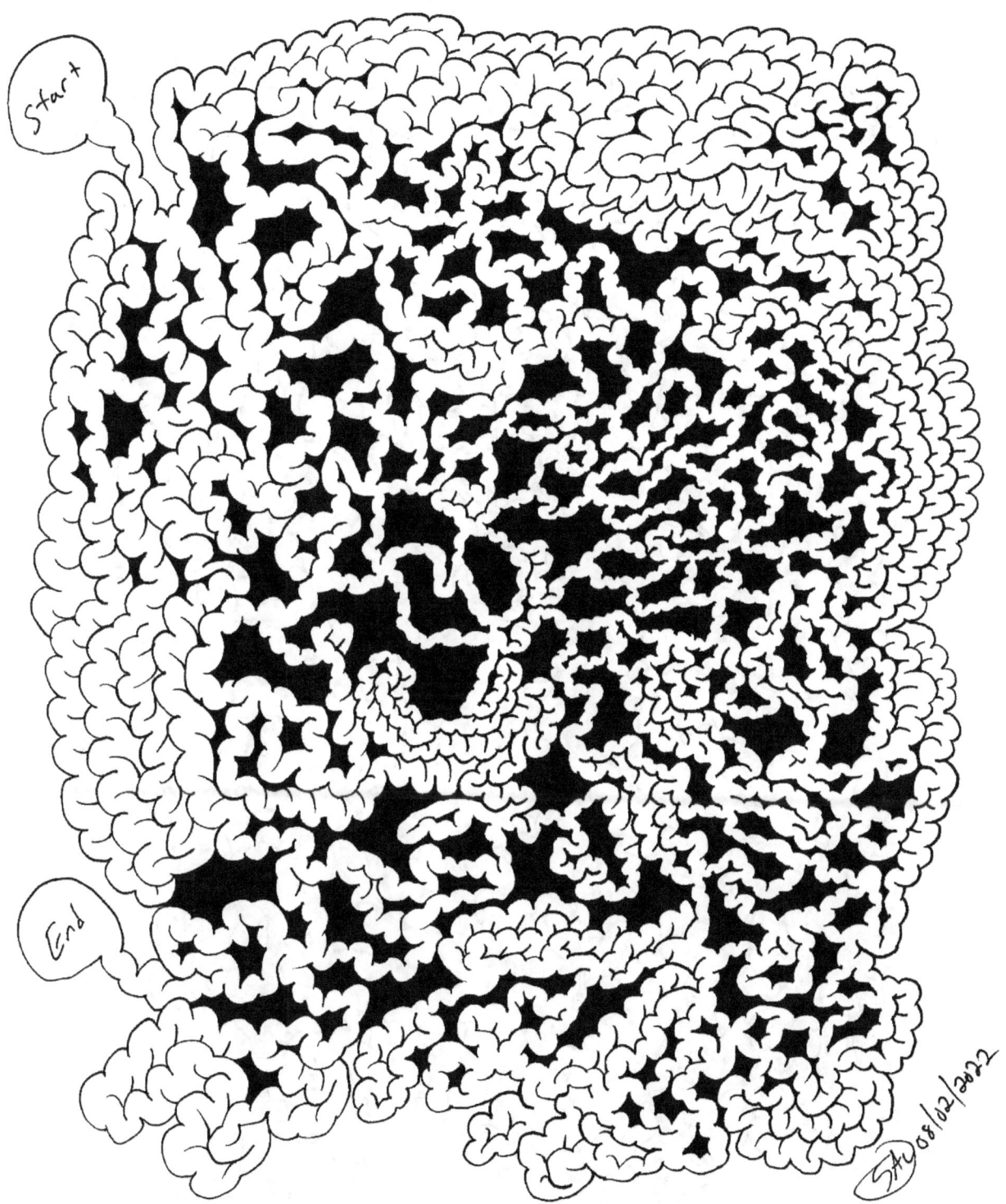

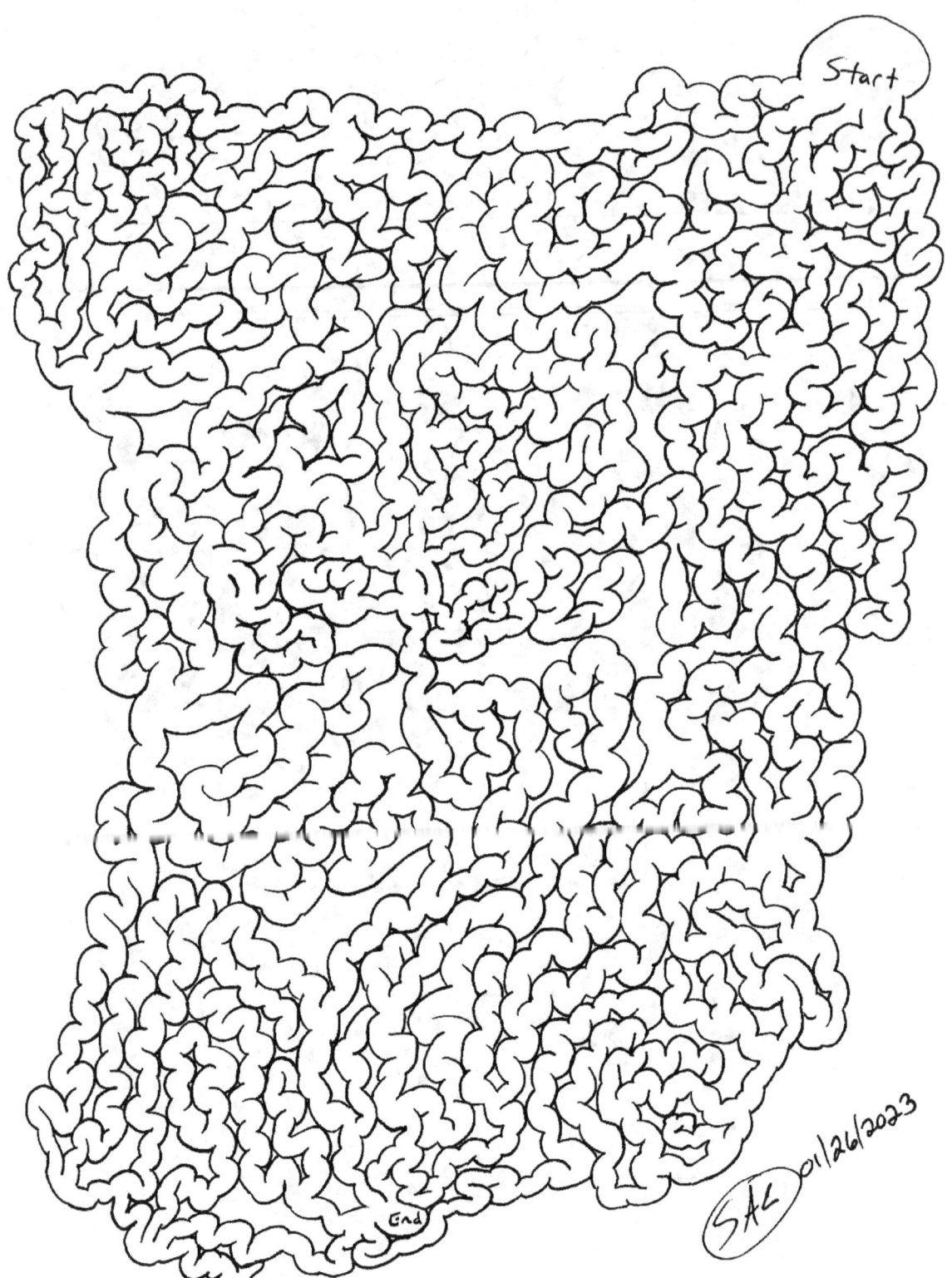

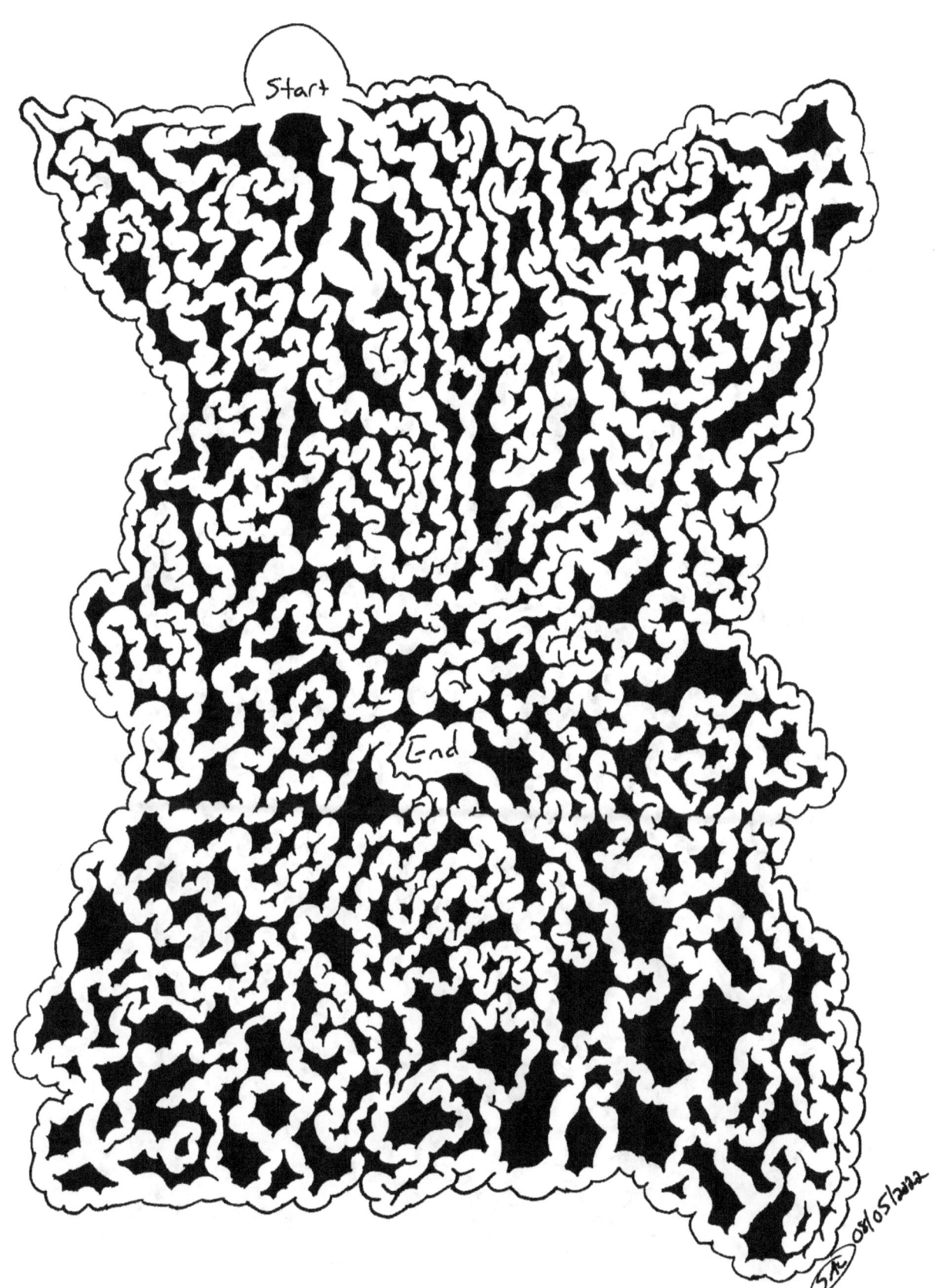

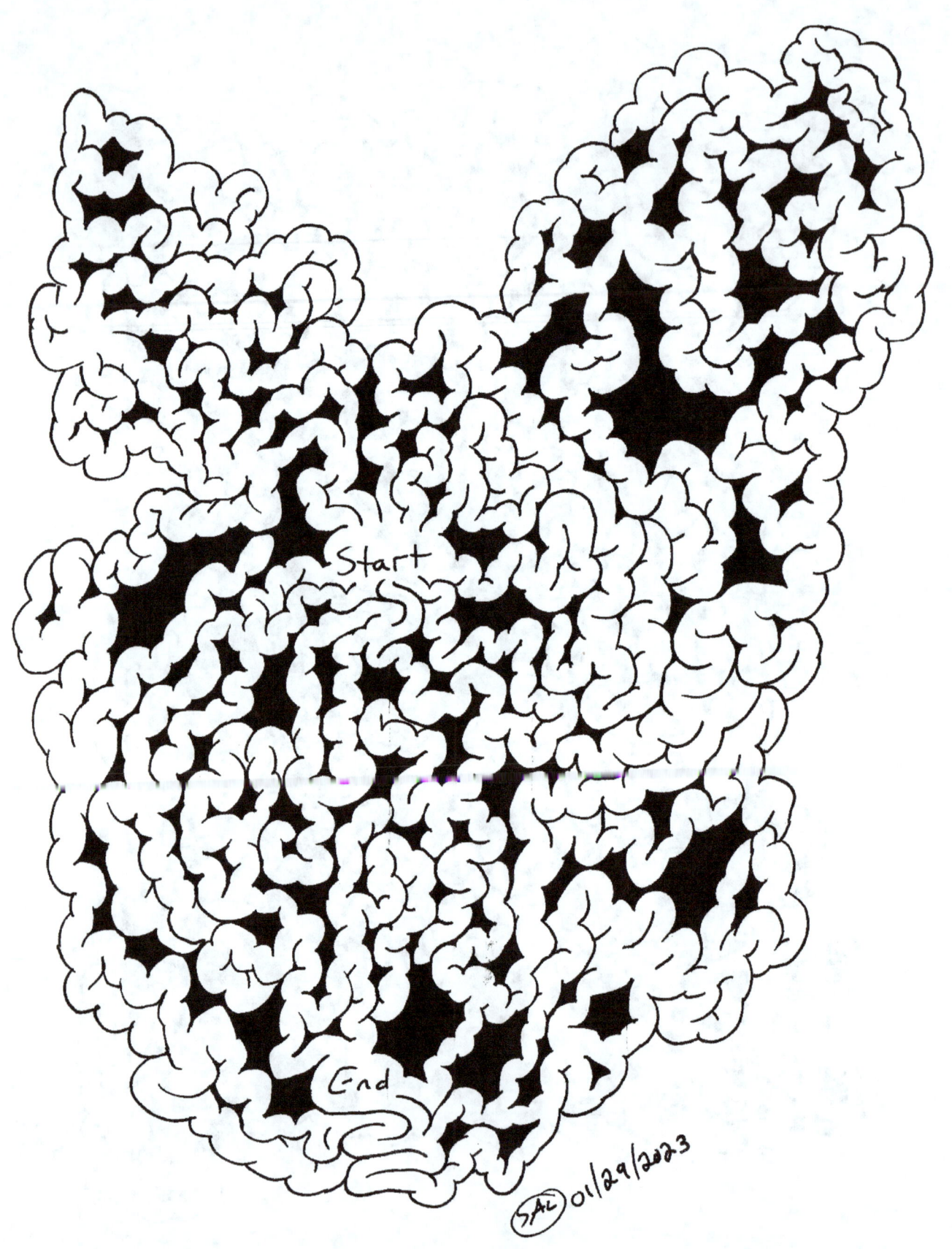

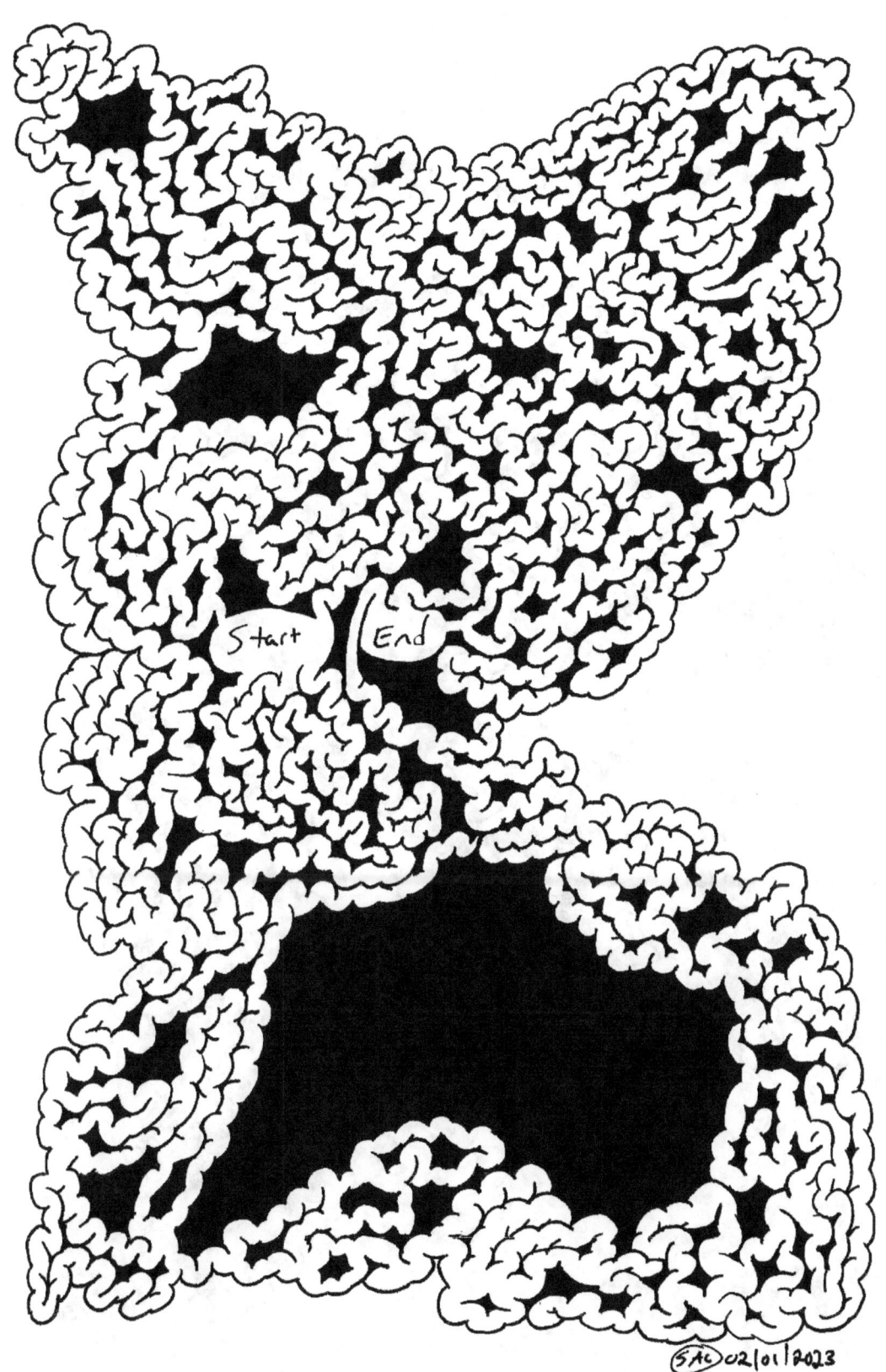

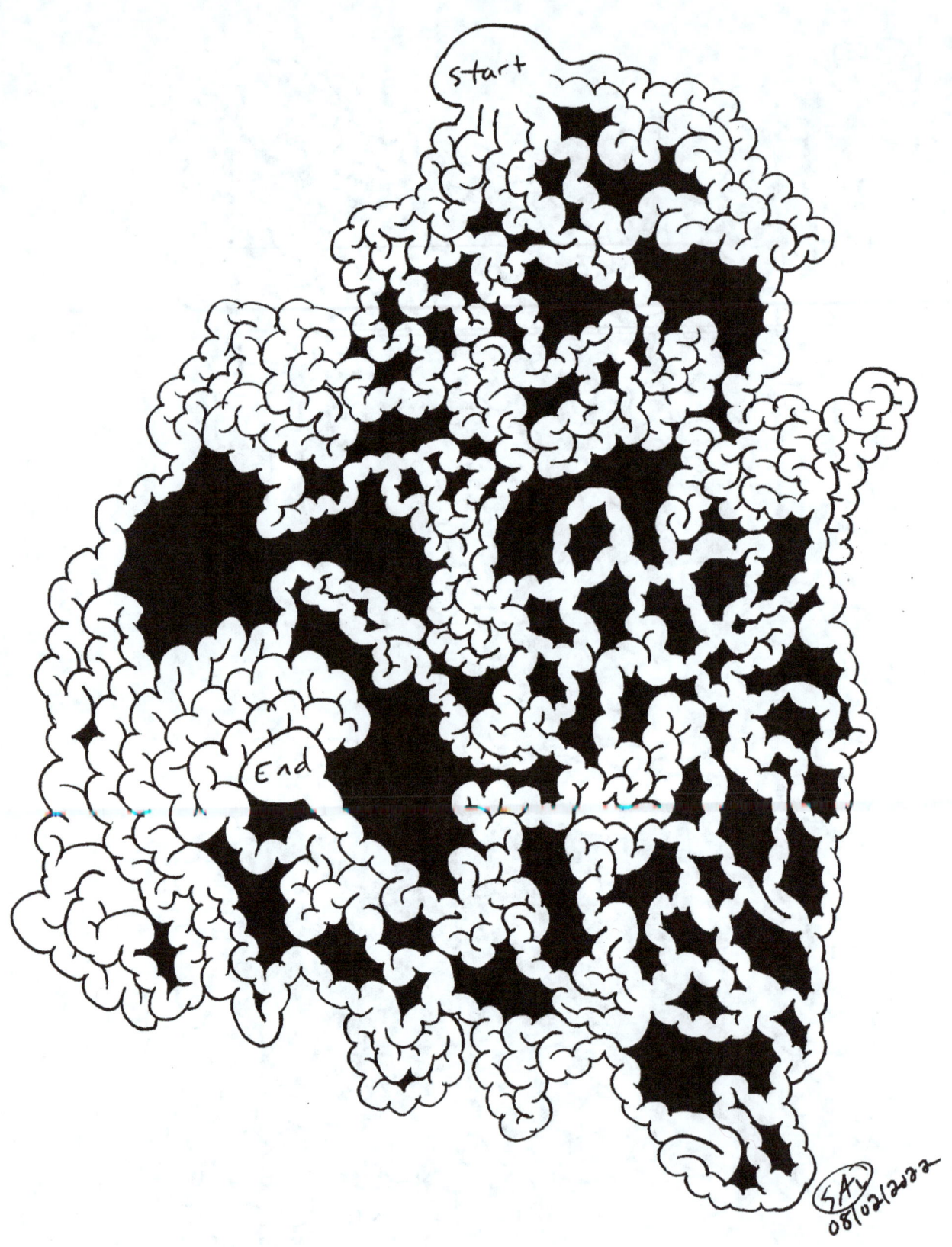

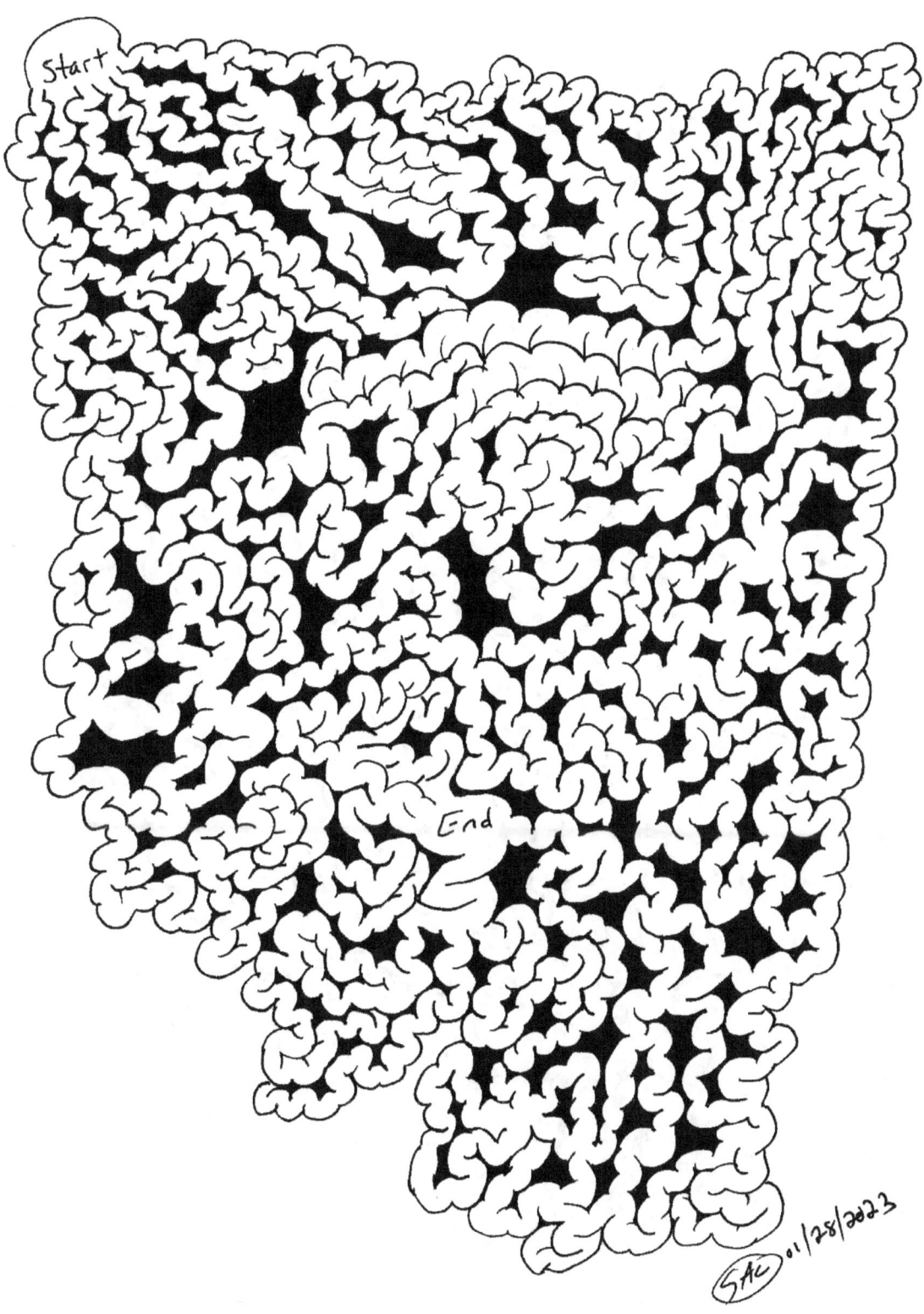

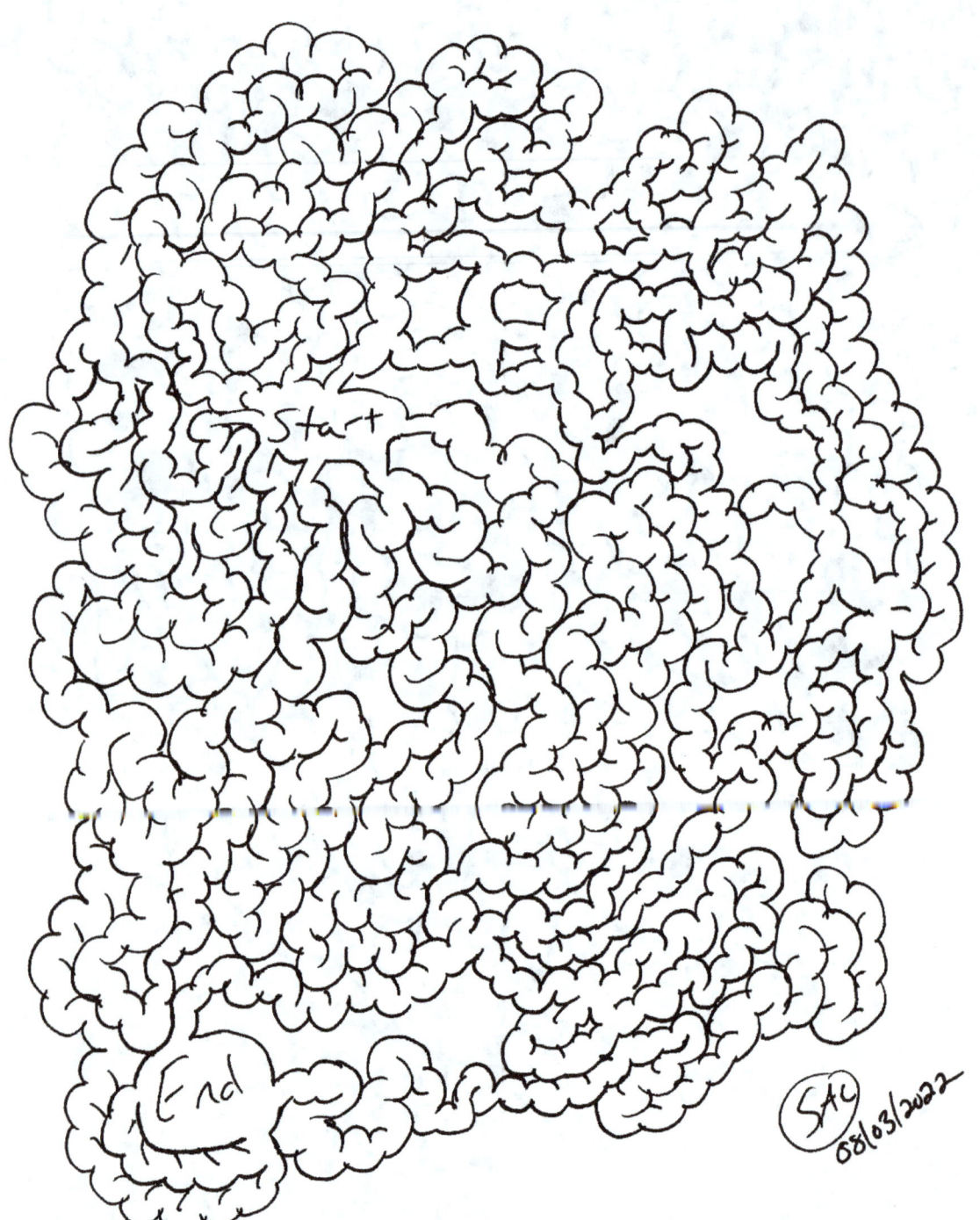

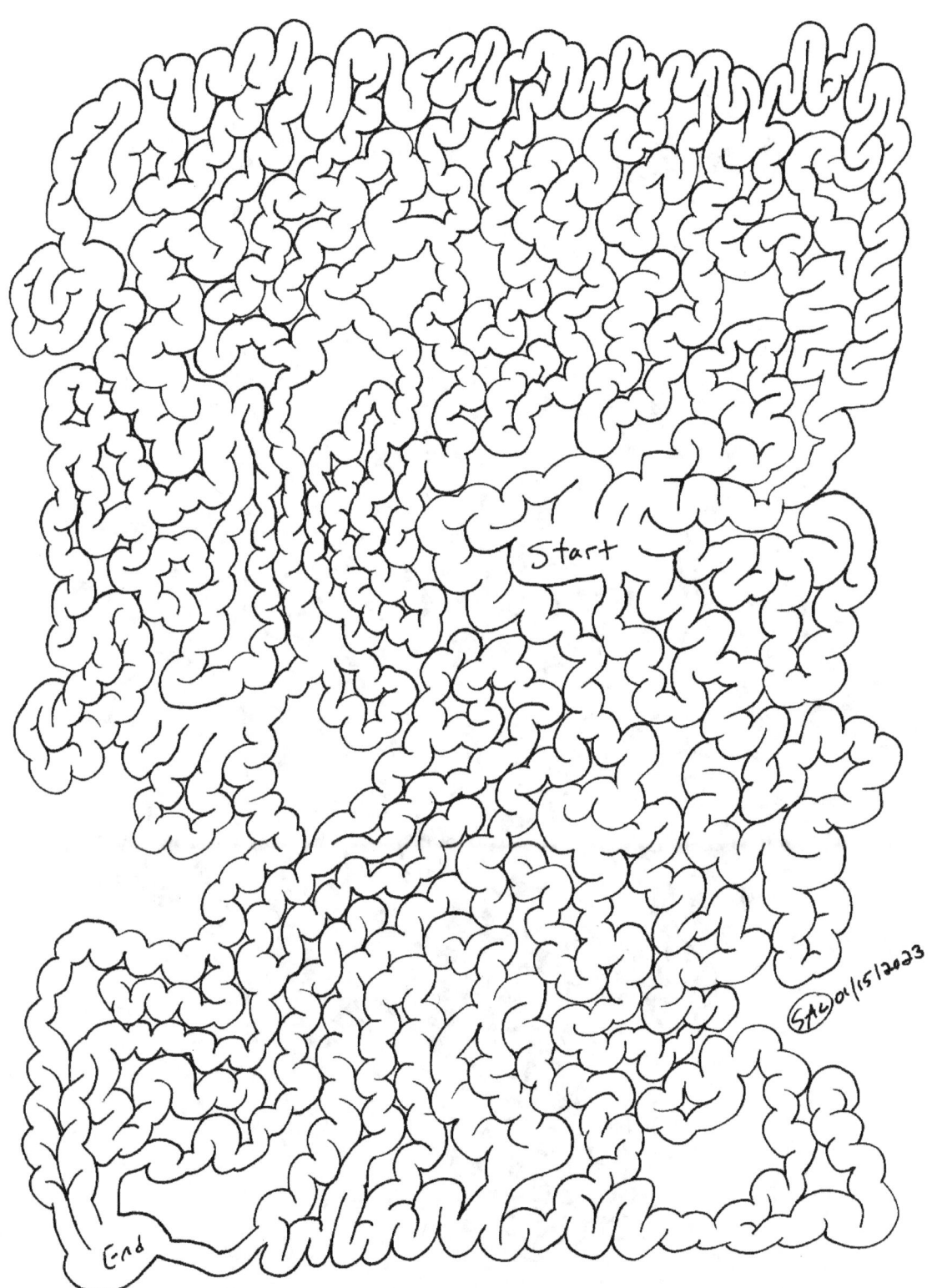

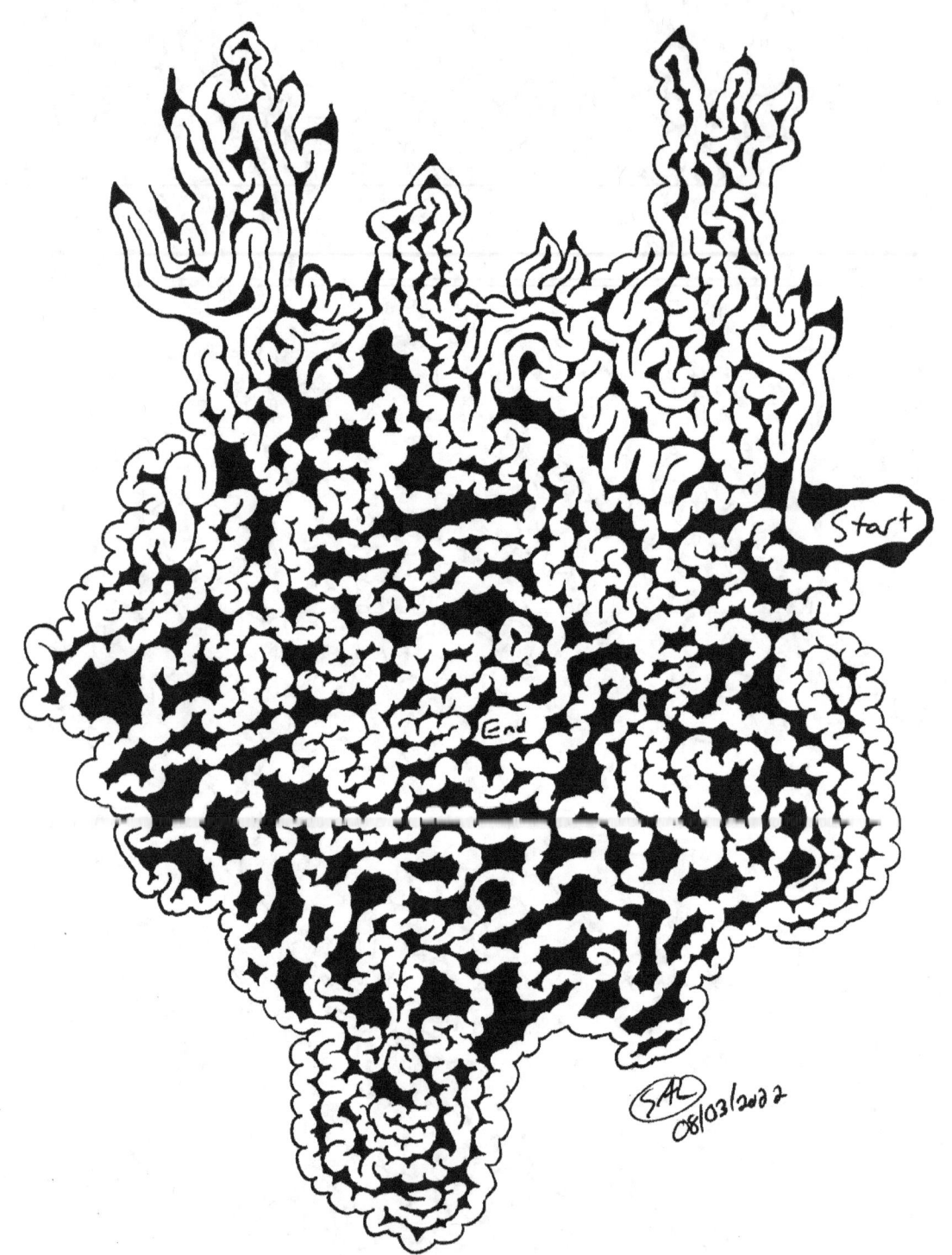

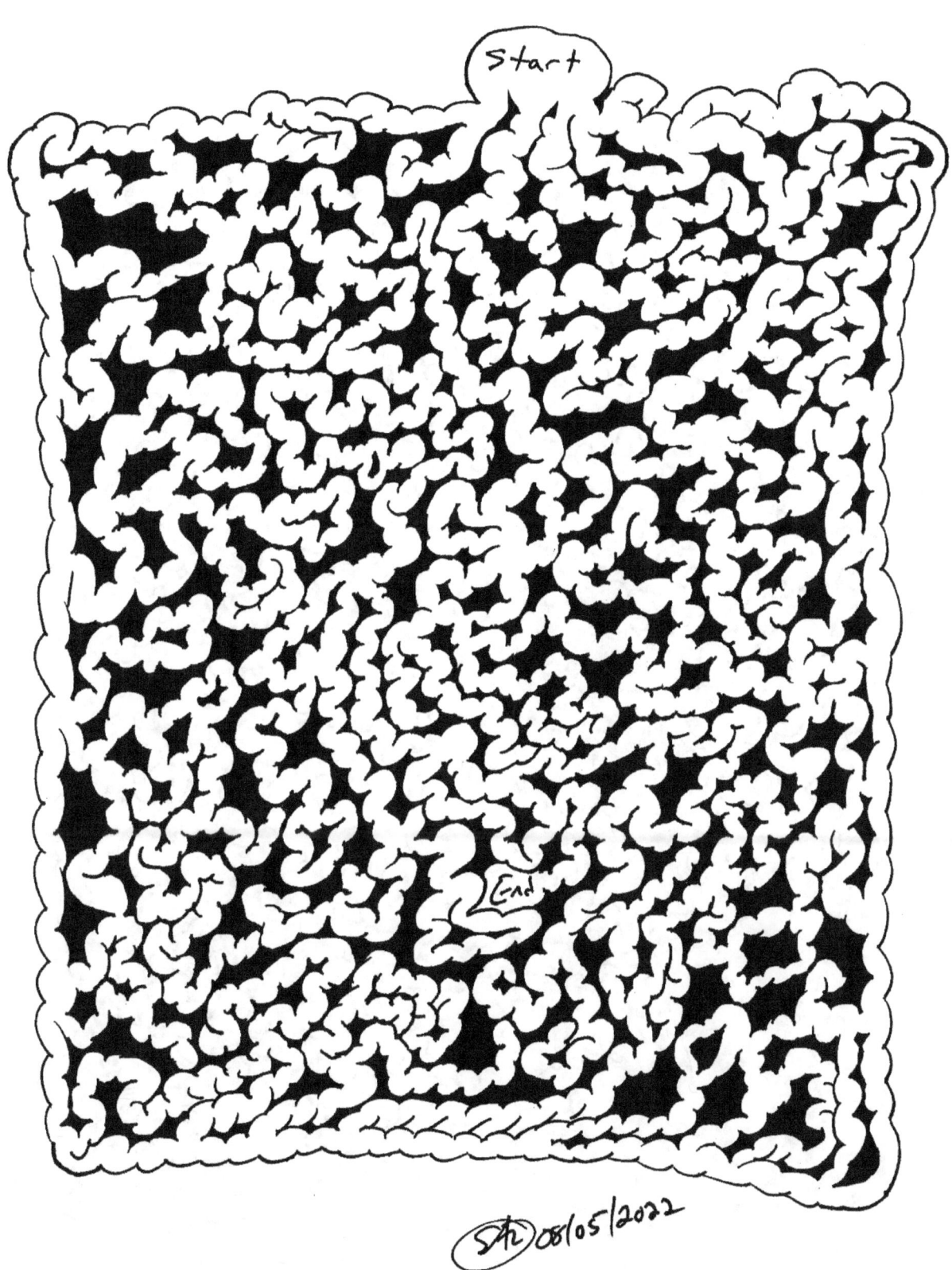

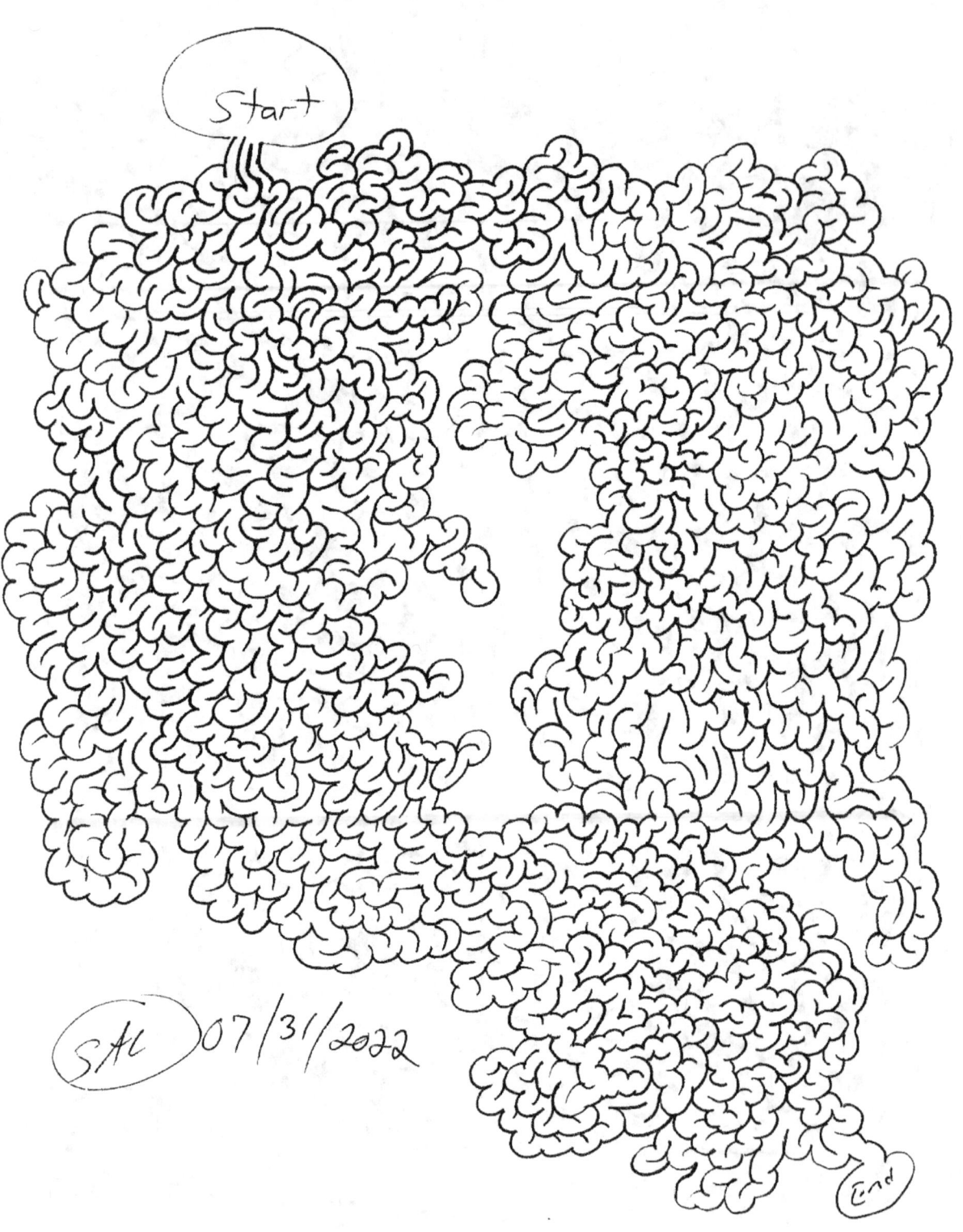

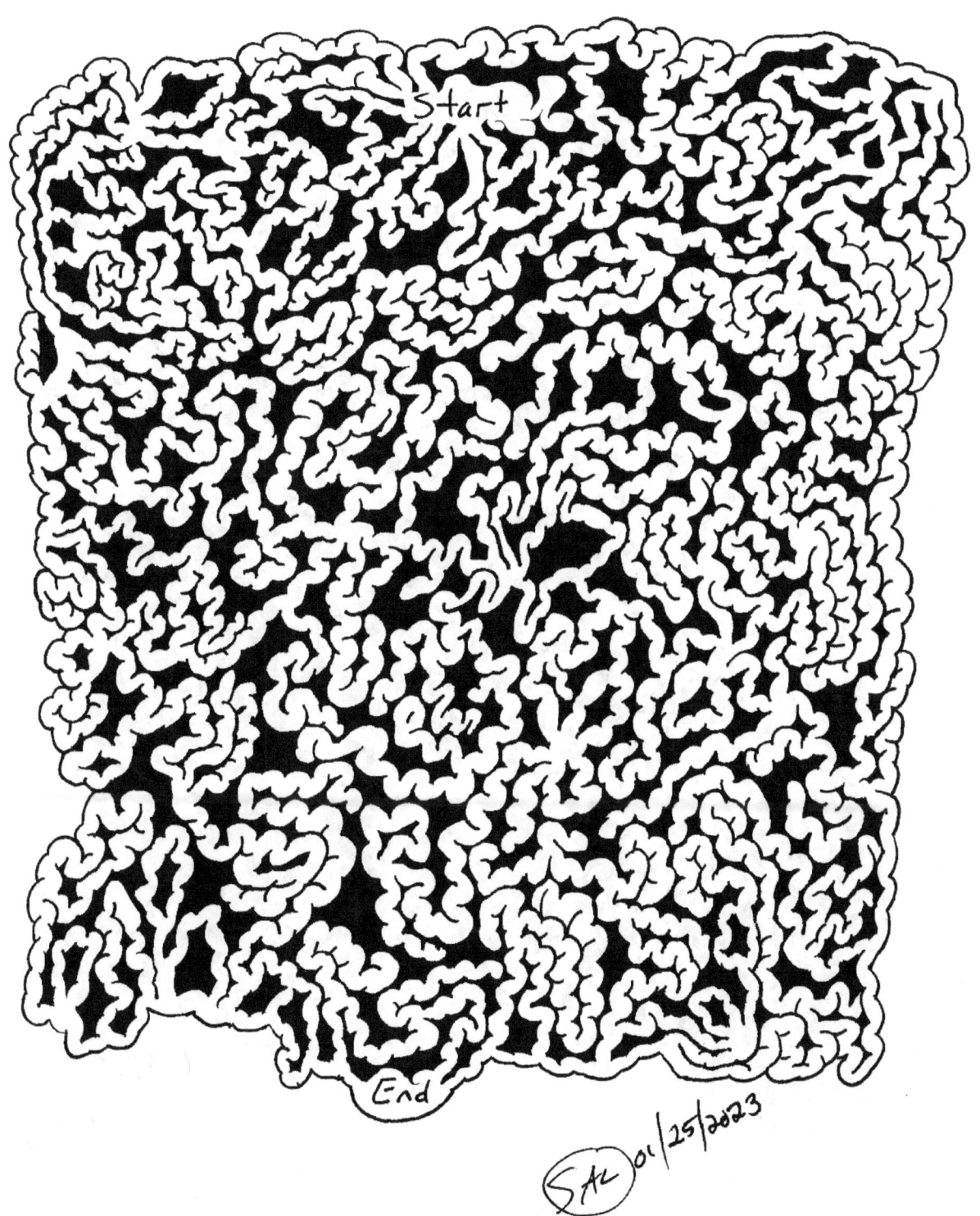

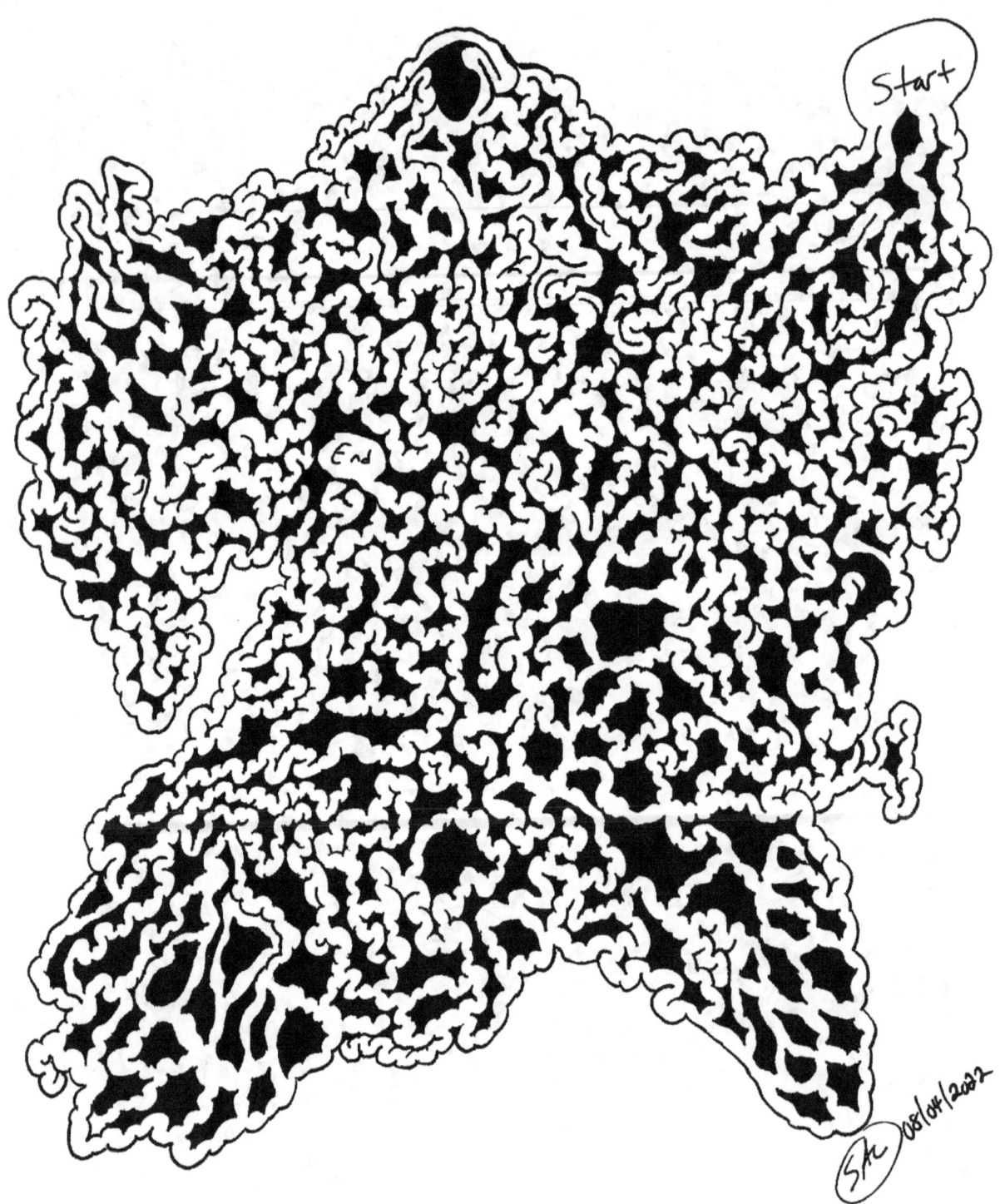

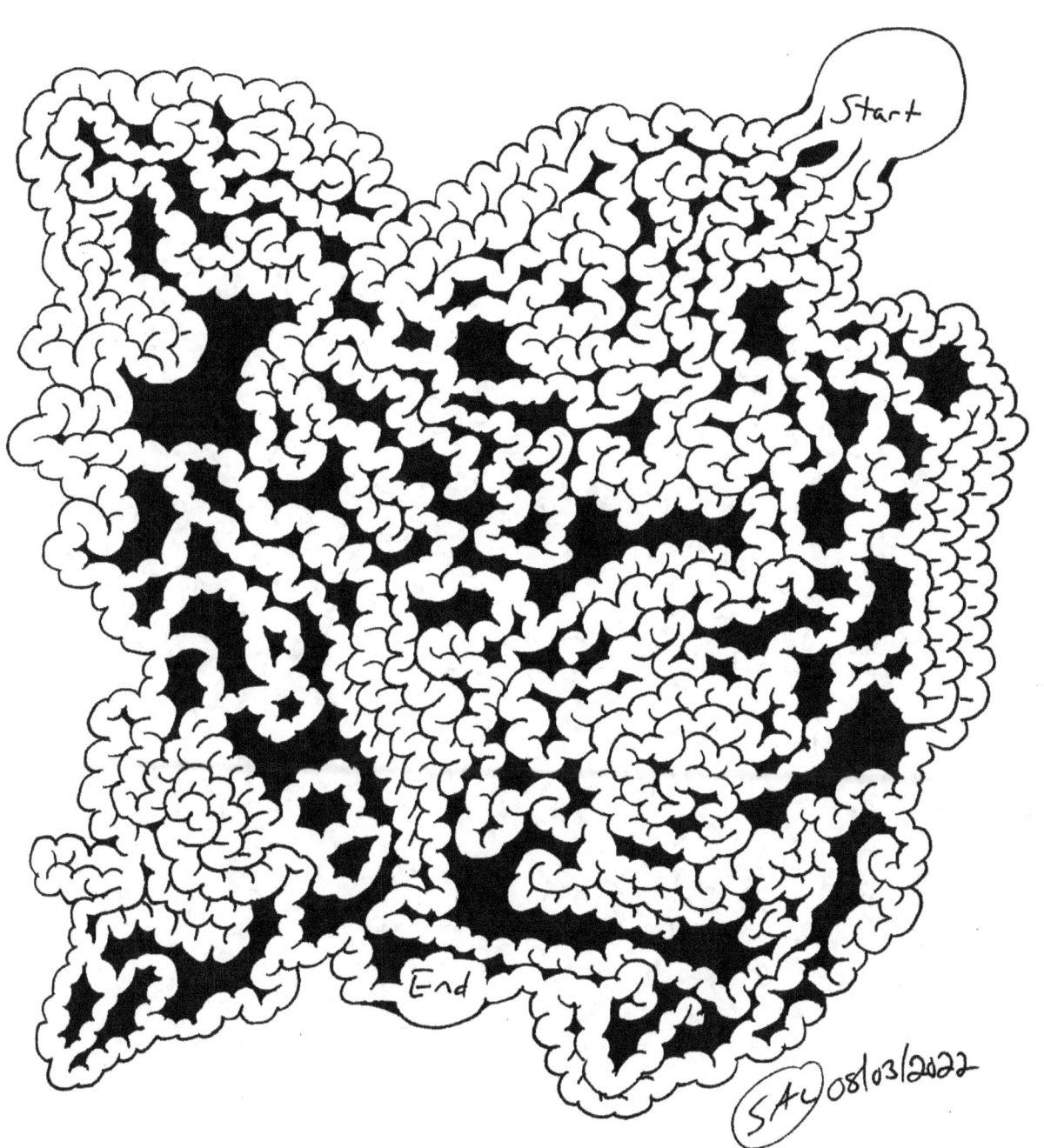

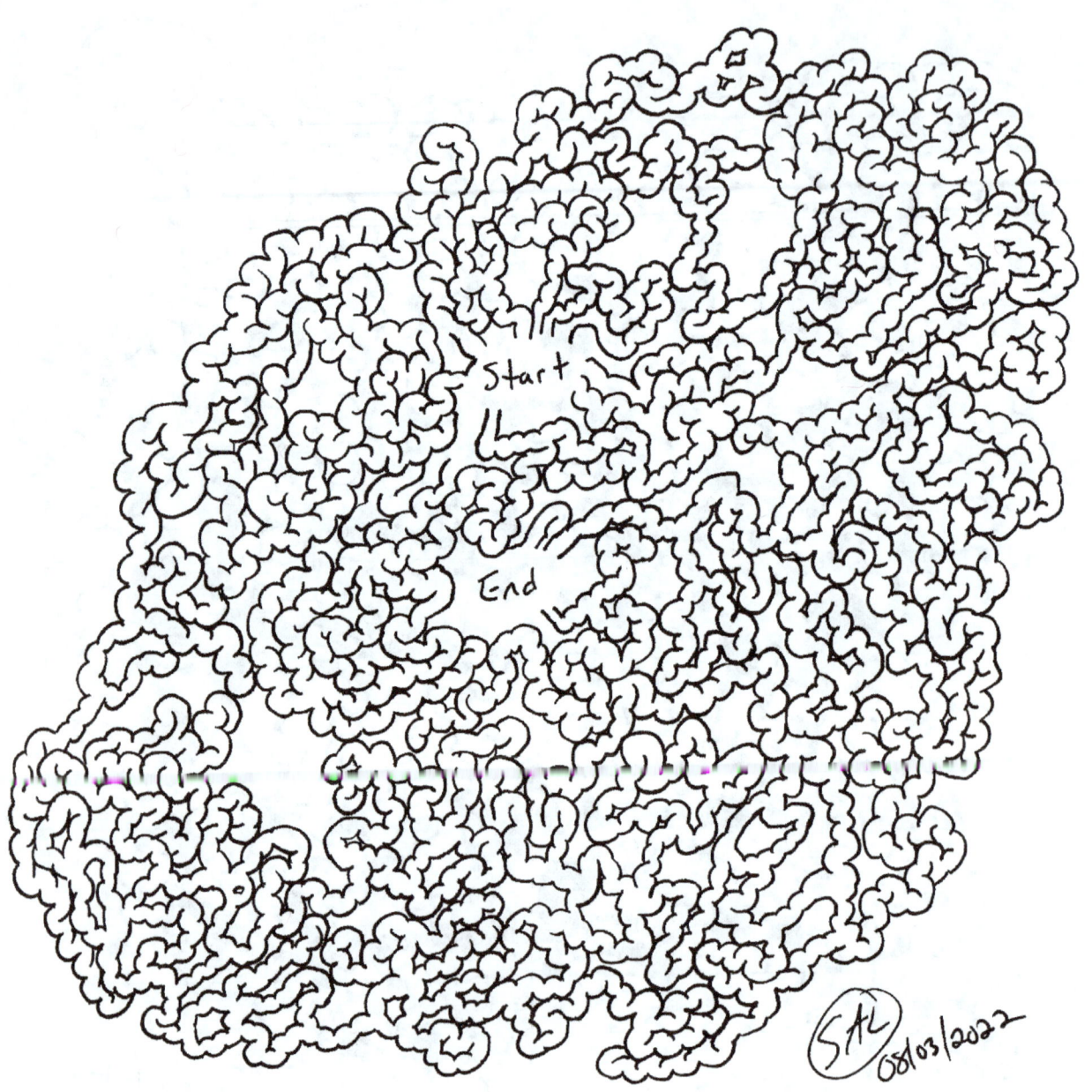

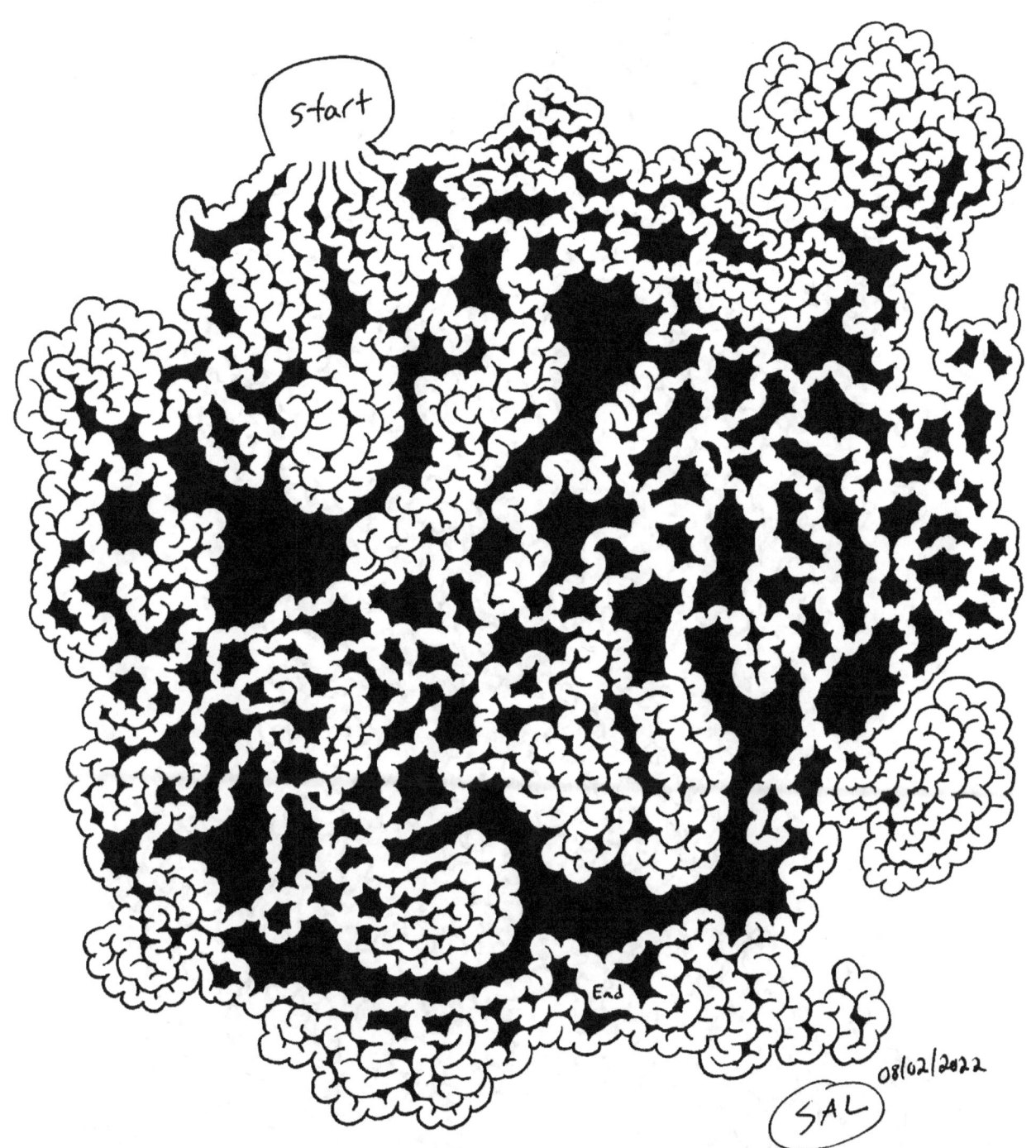

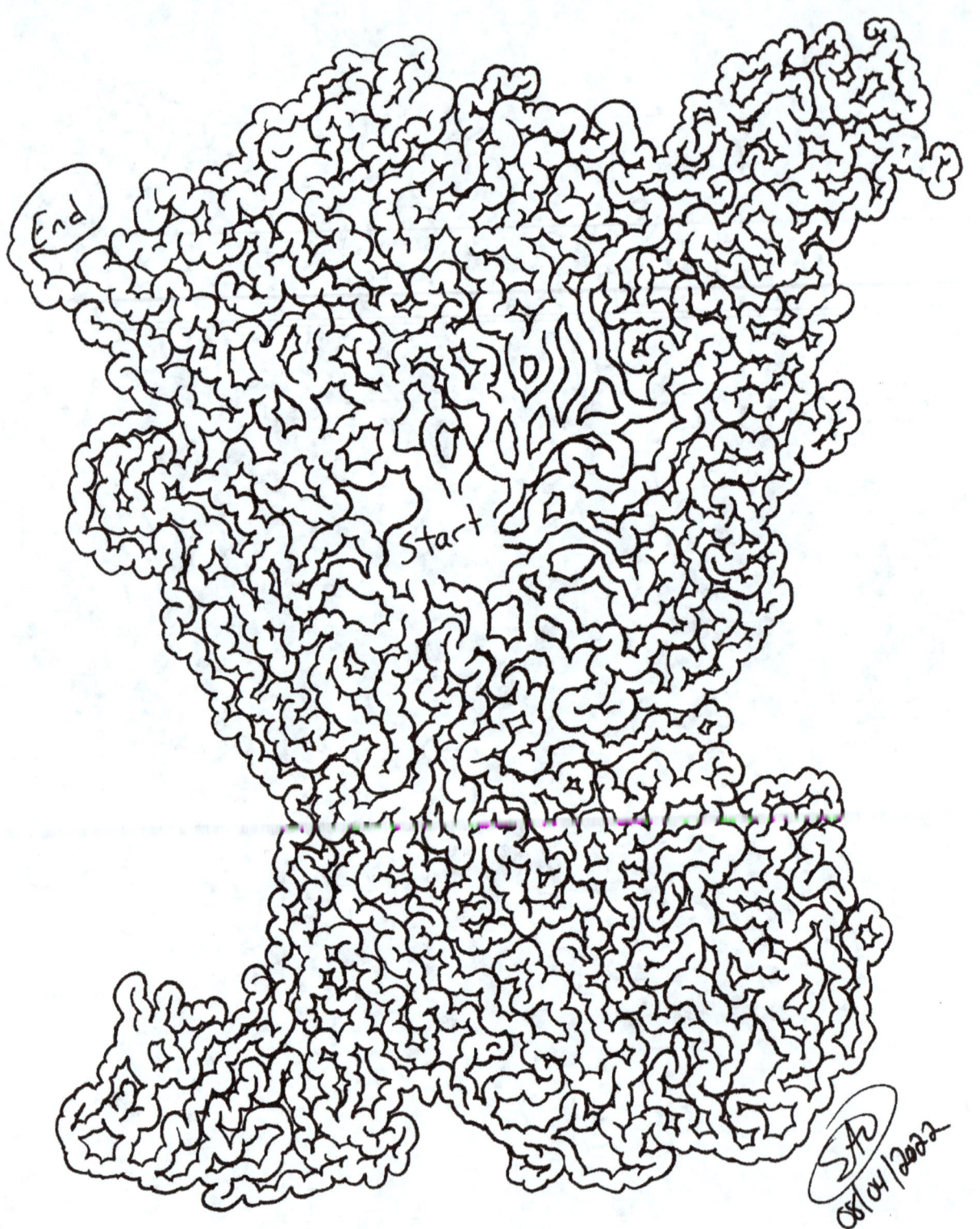

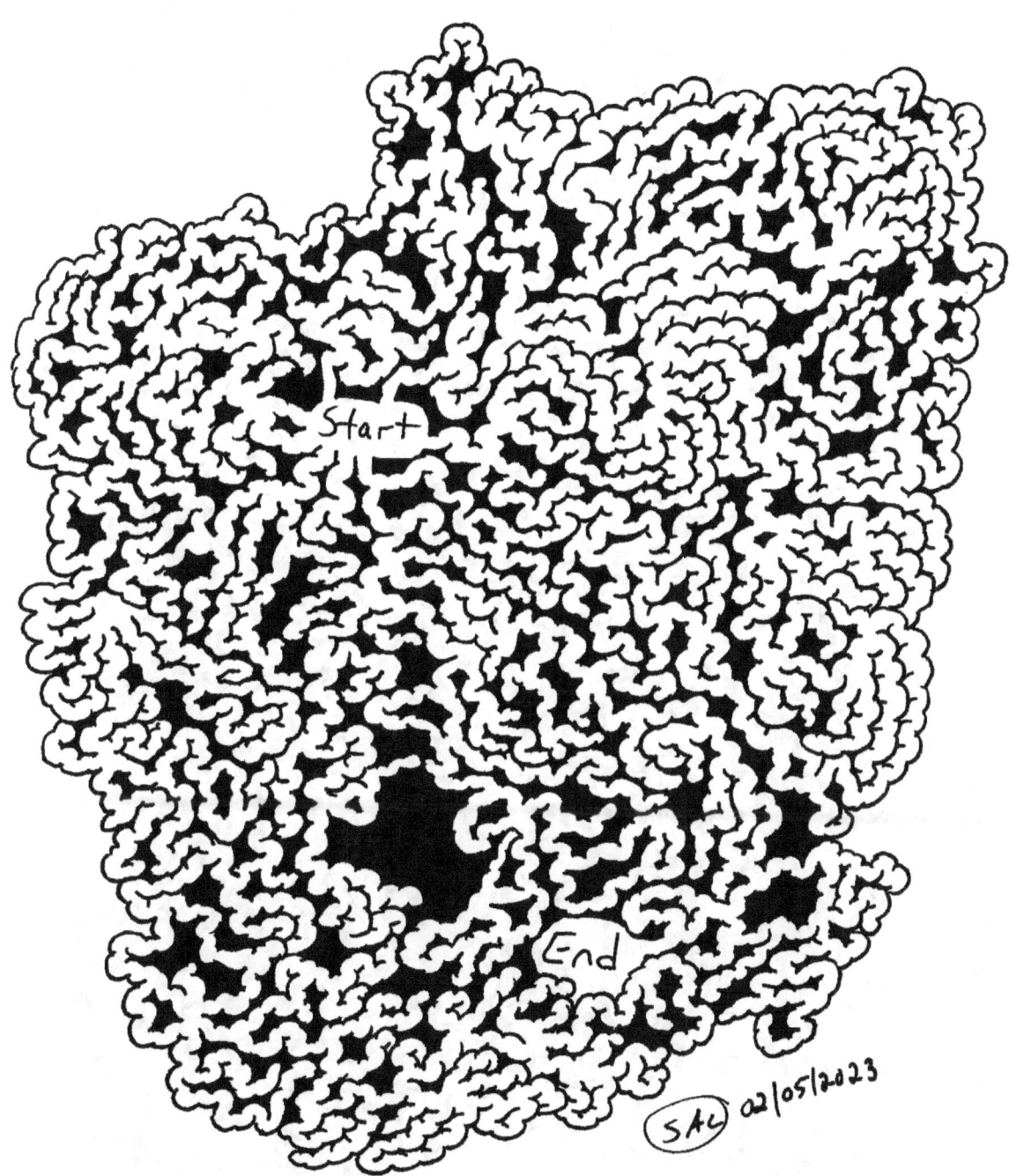

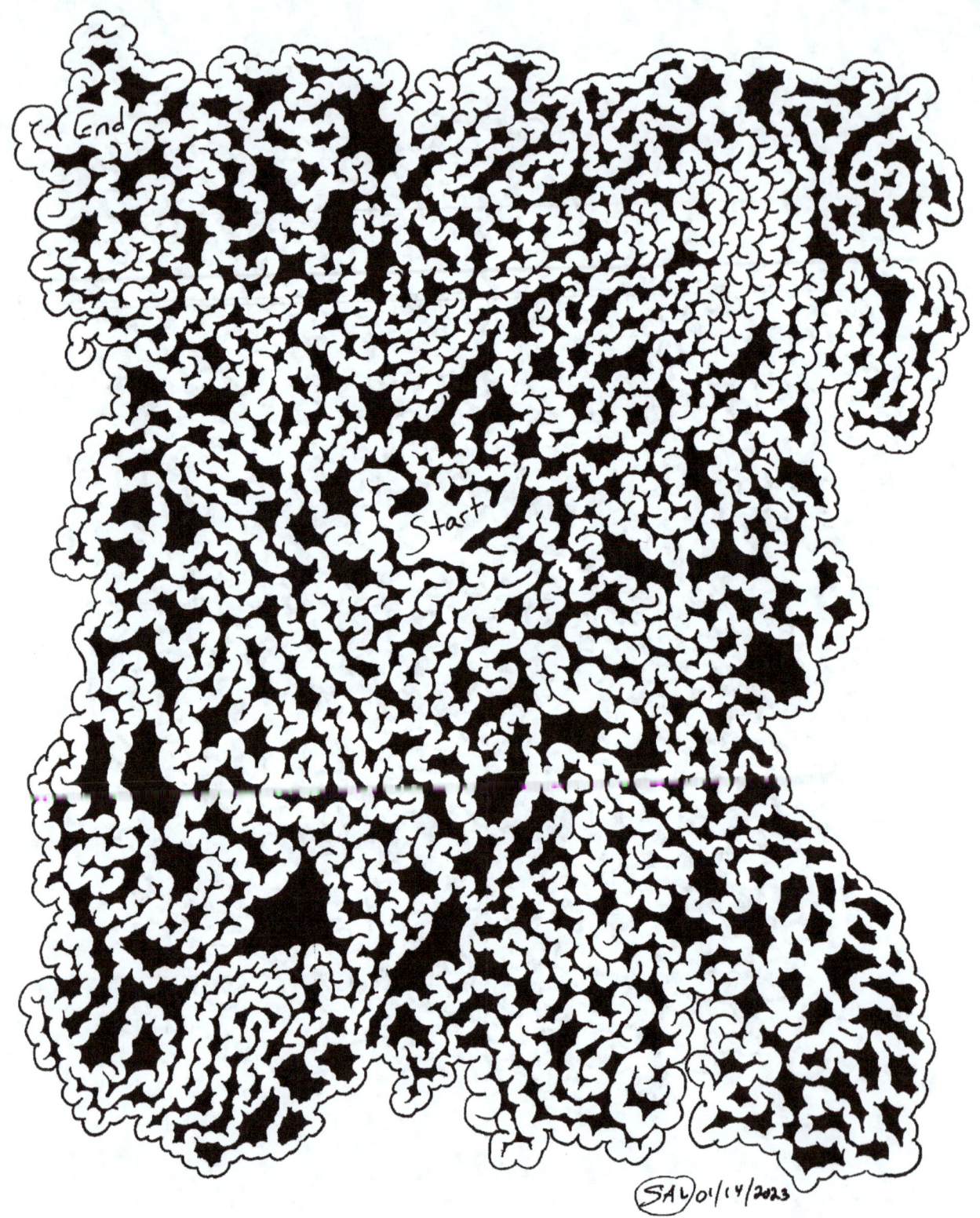

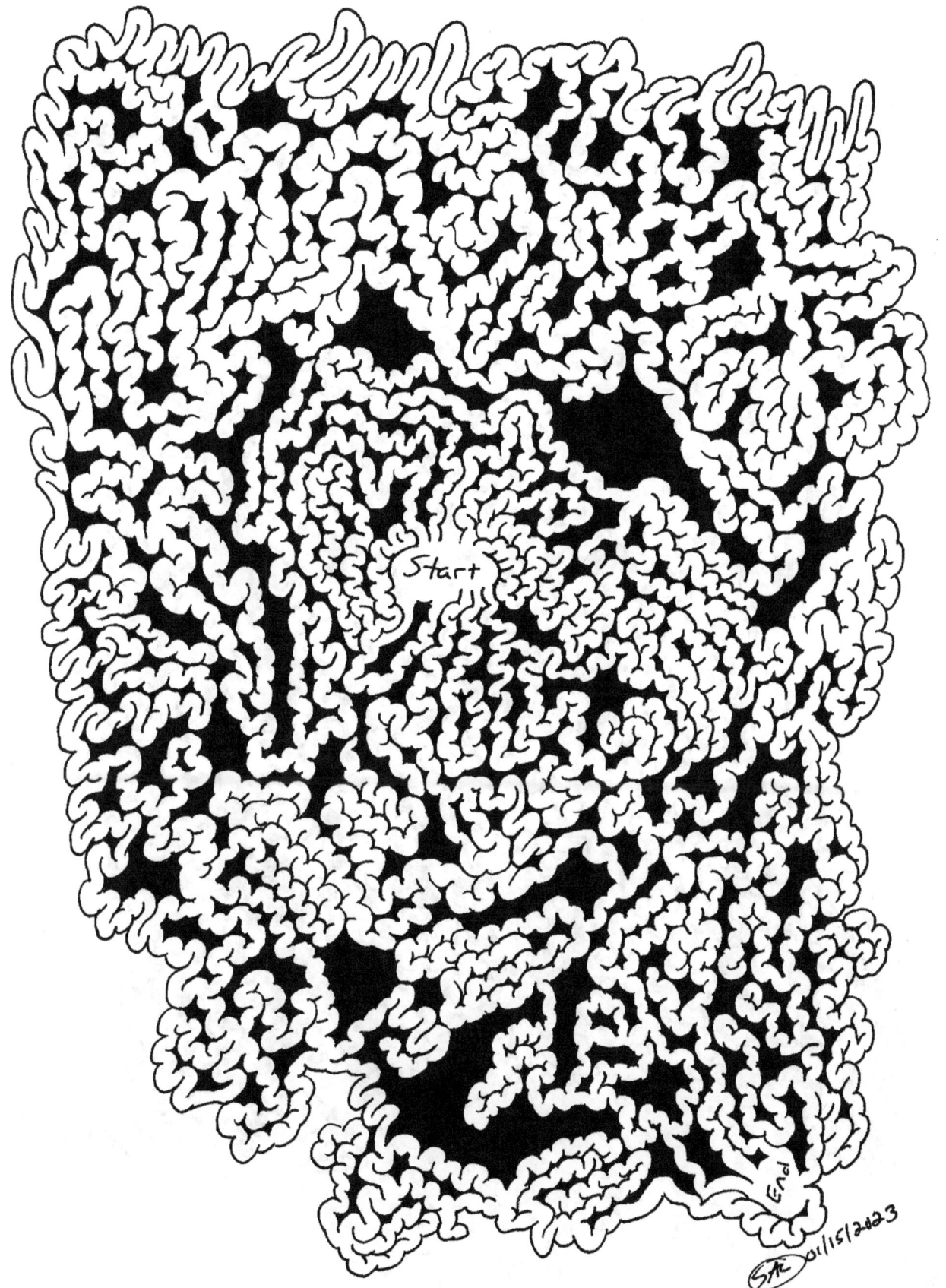

Start

End

01/15/2023

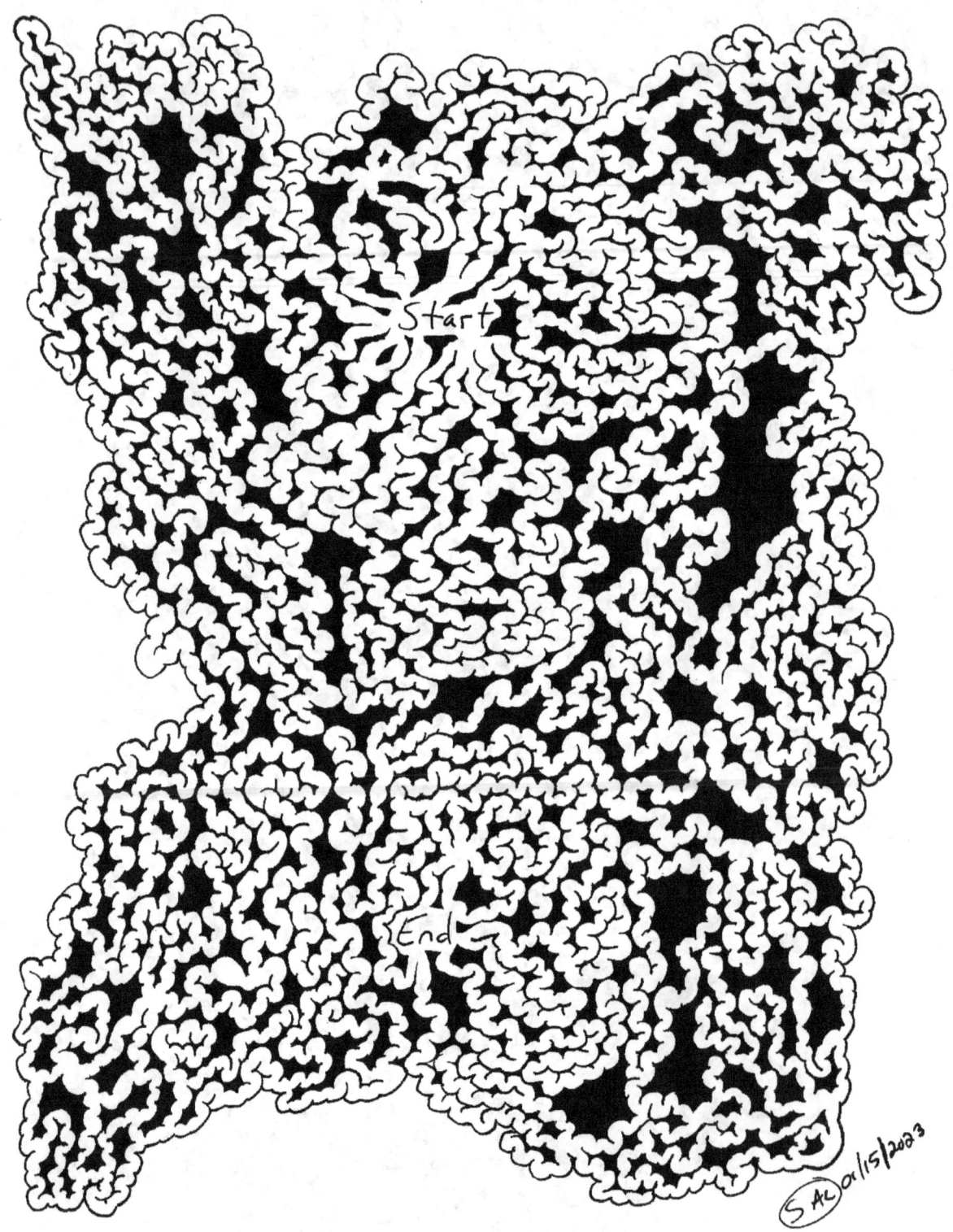

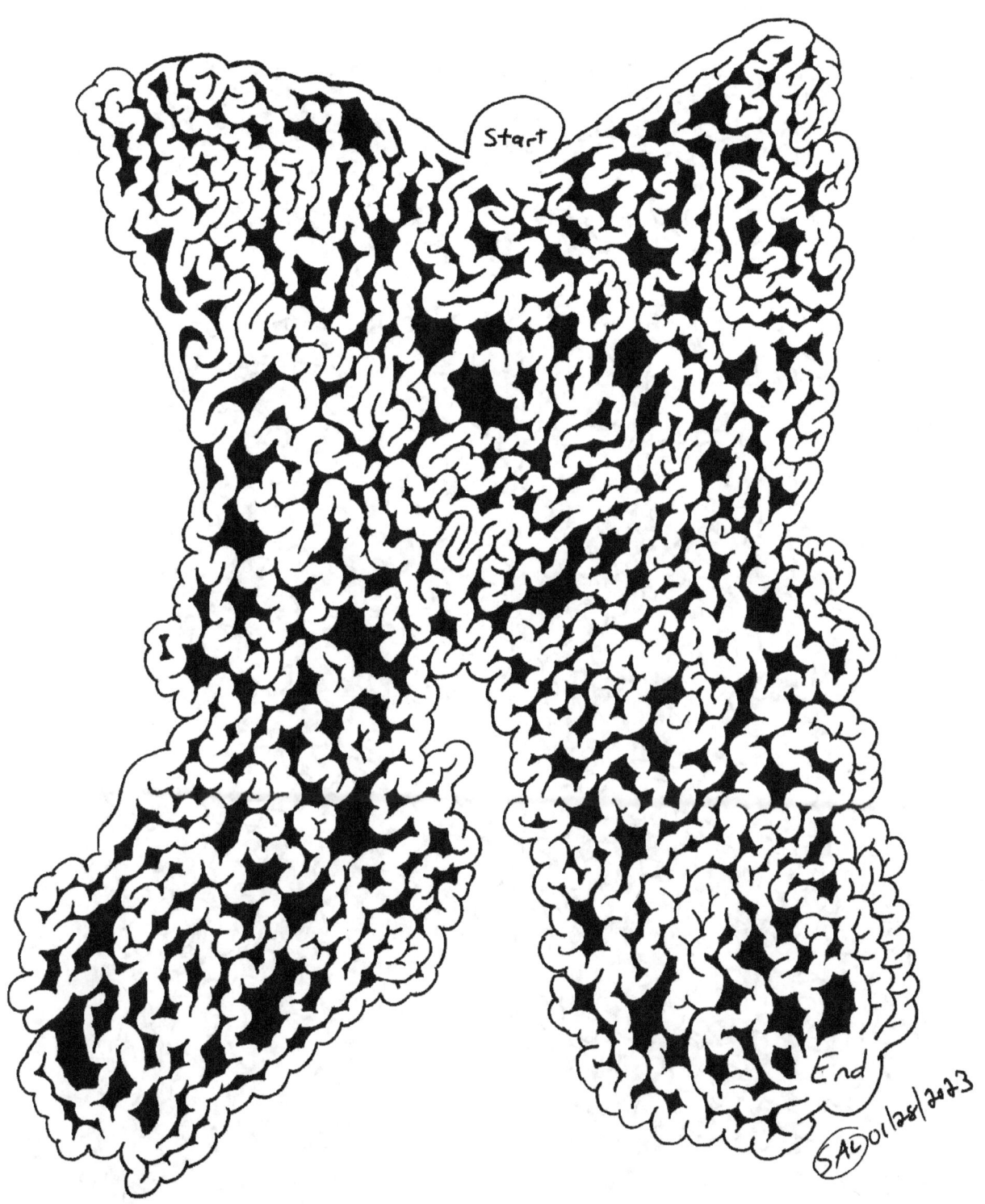

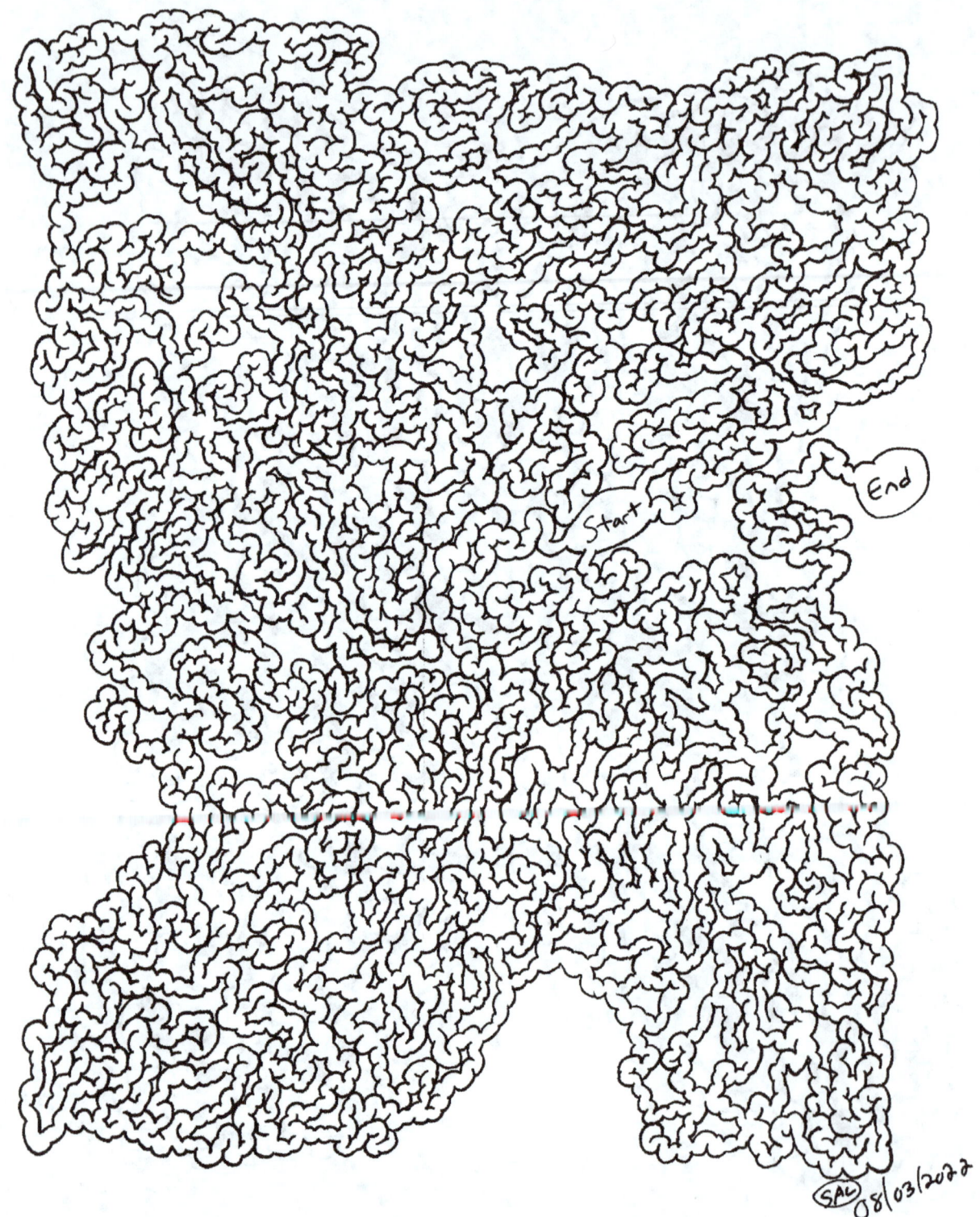

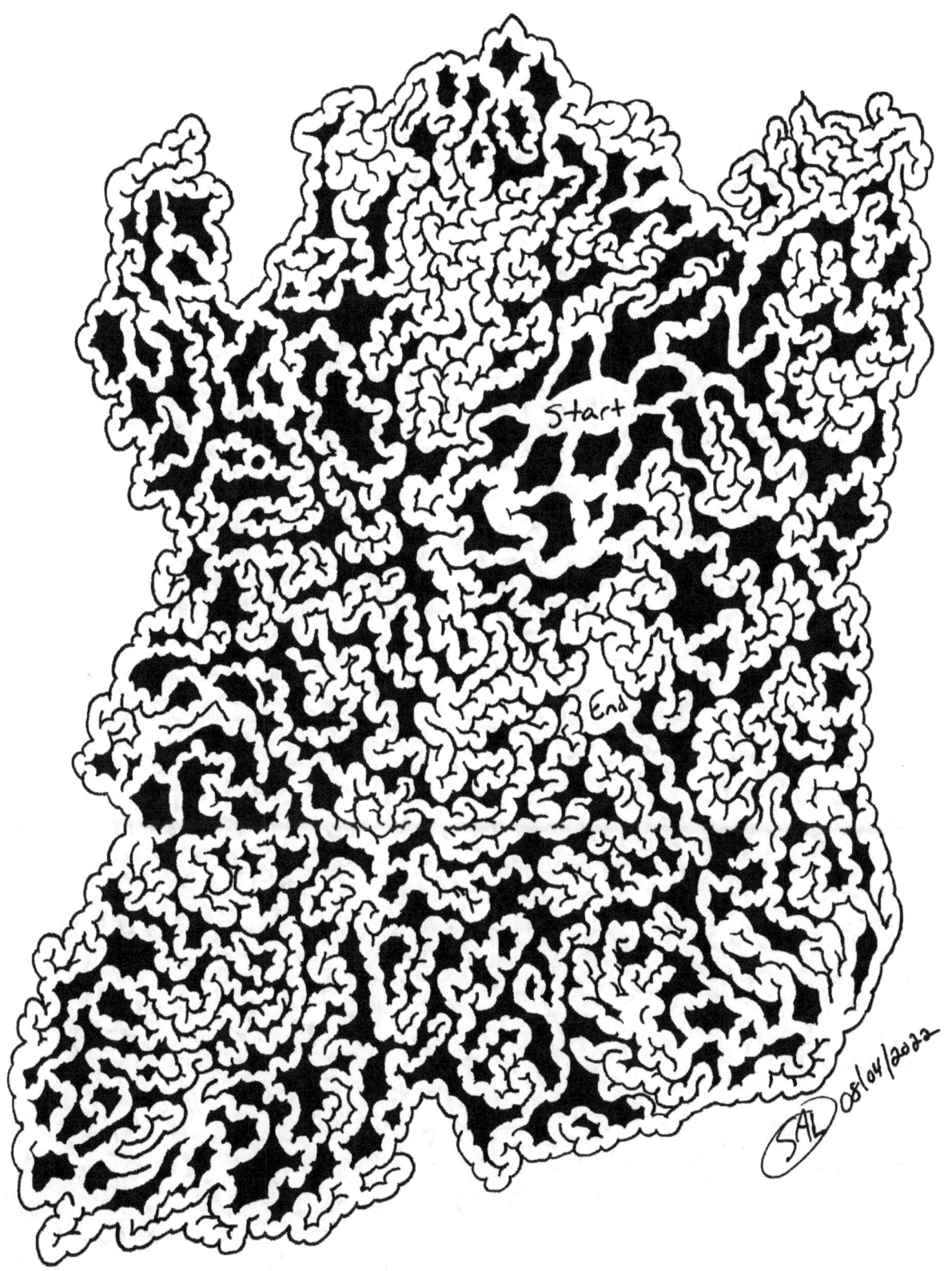

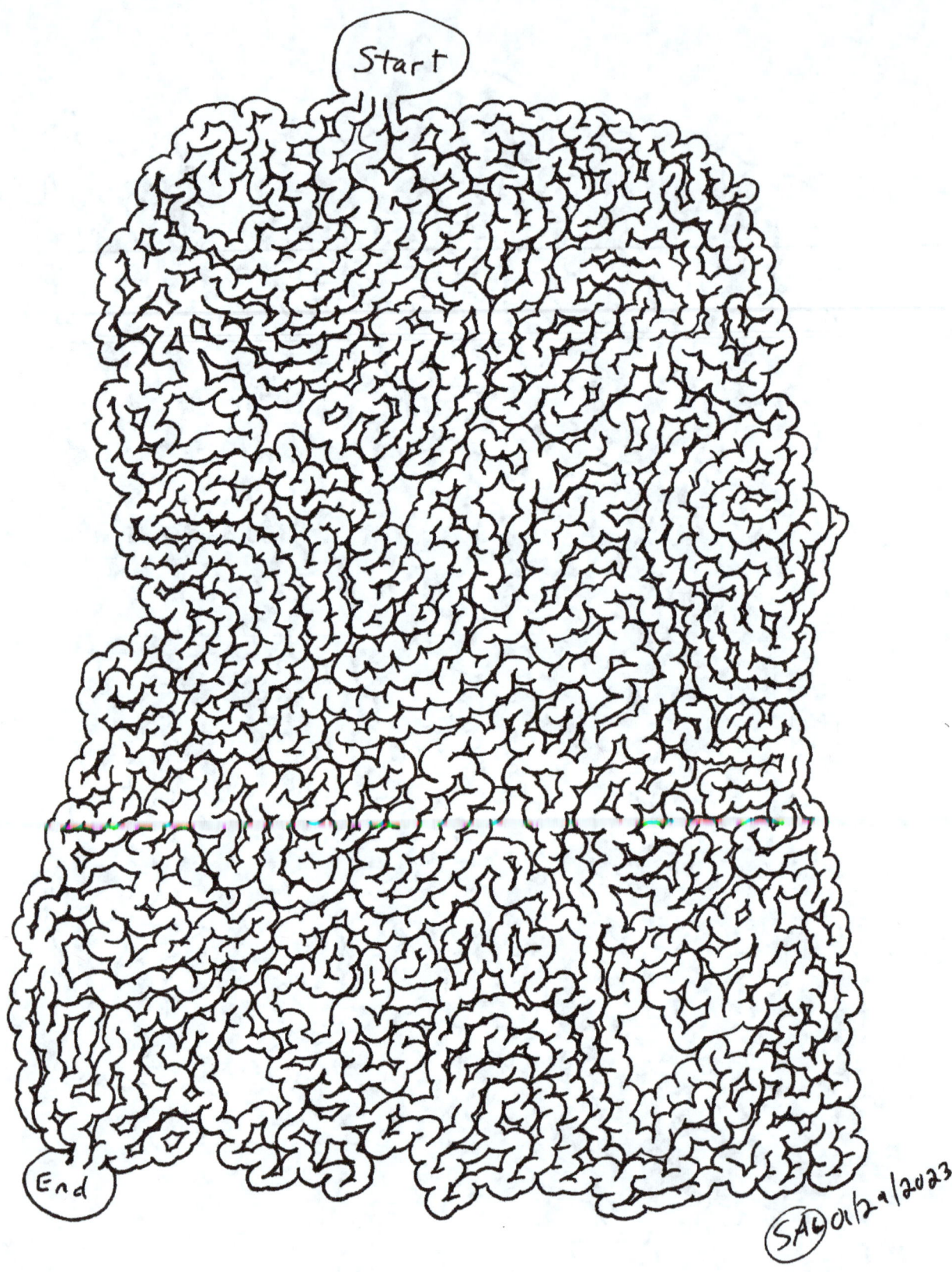

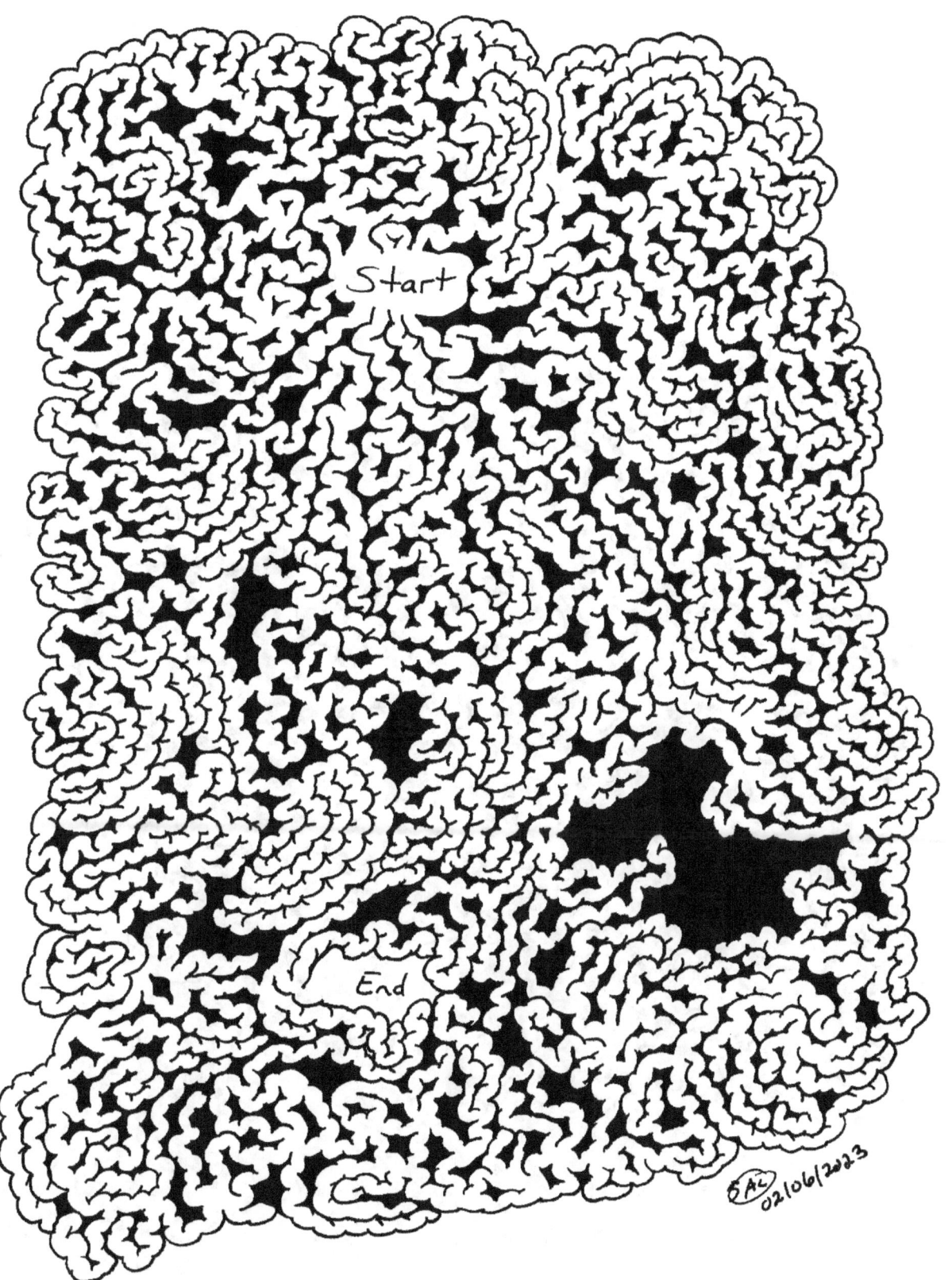

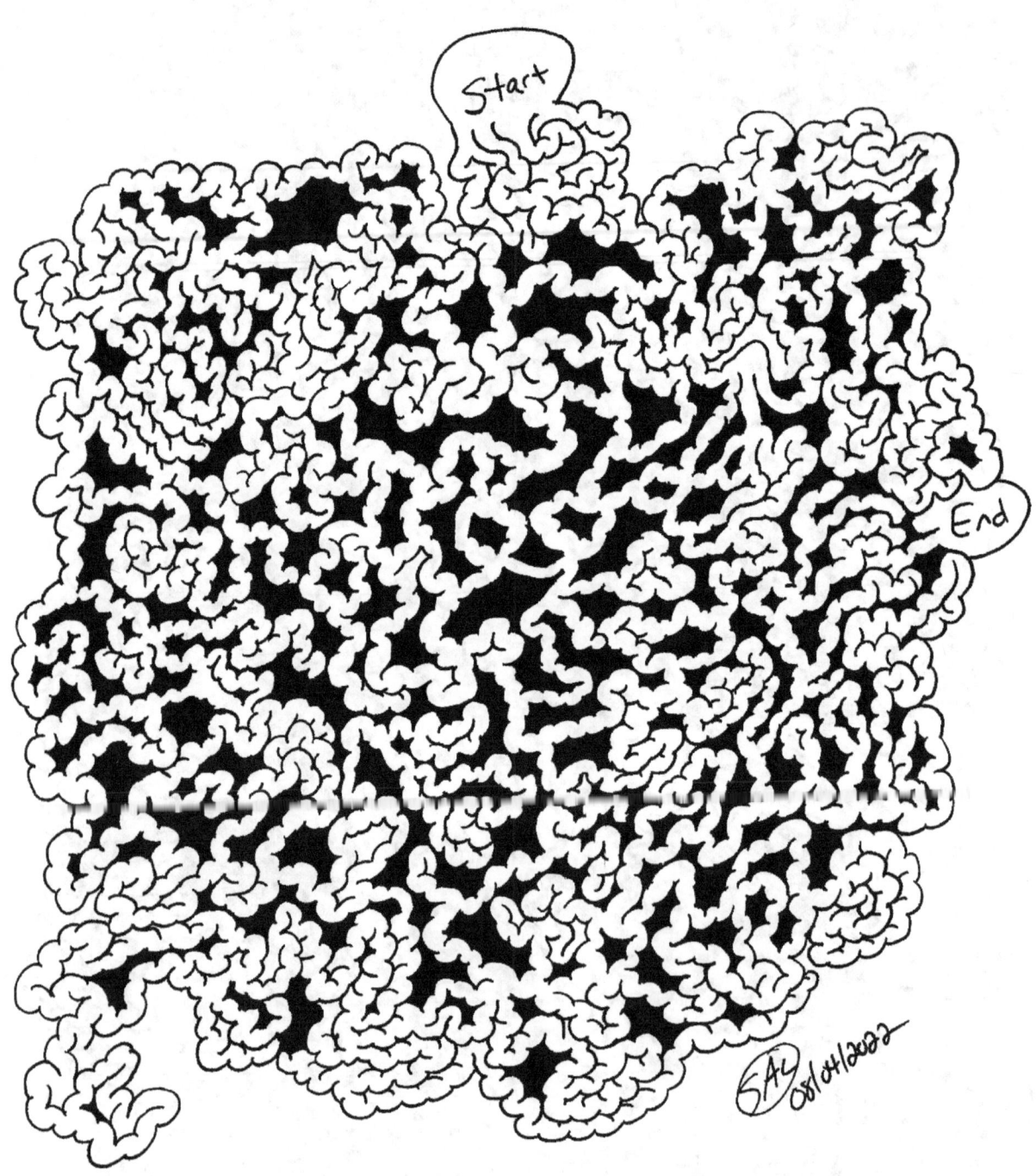

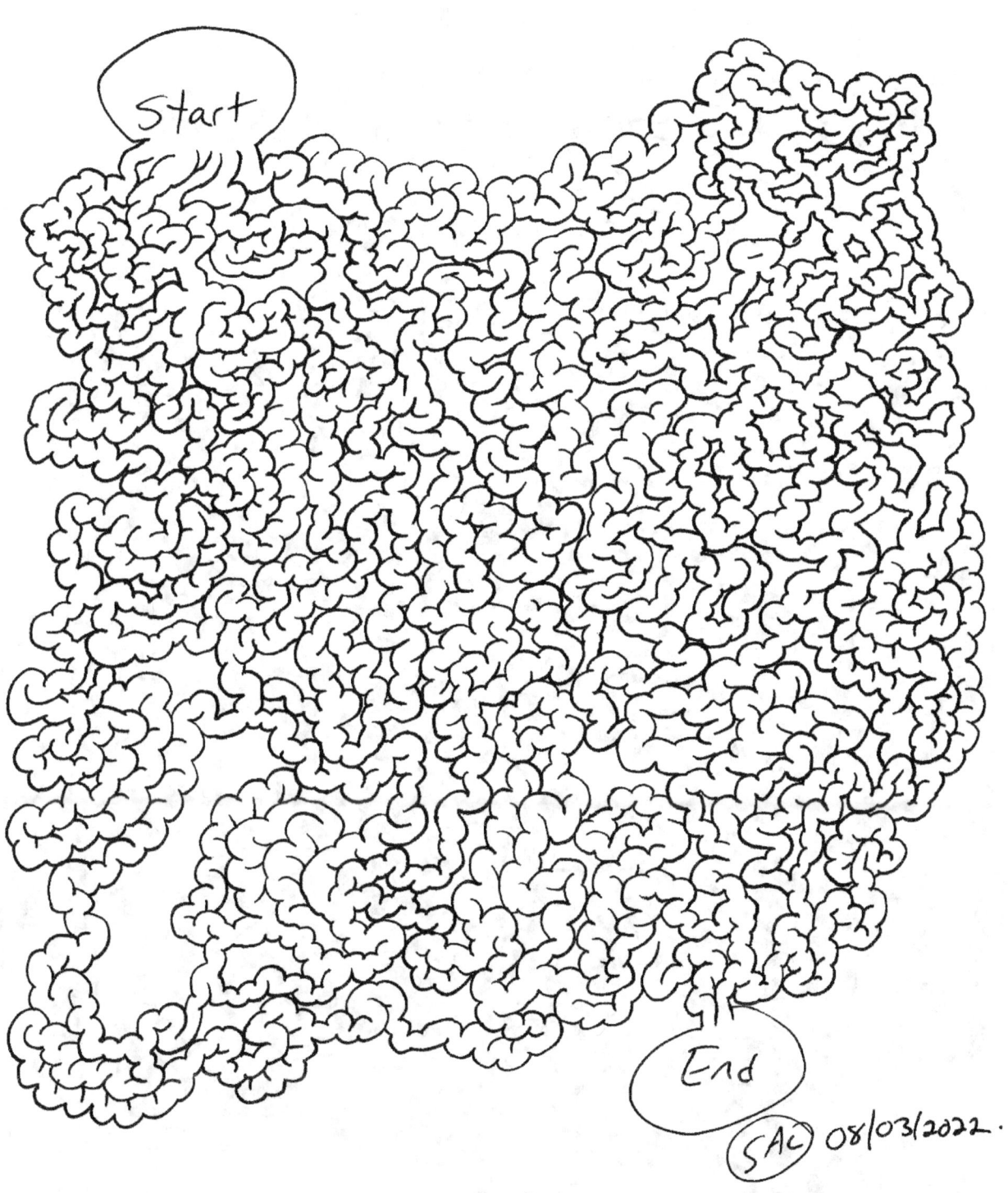

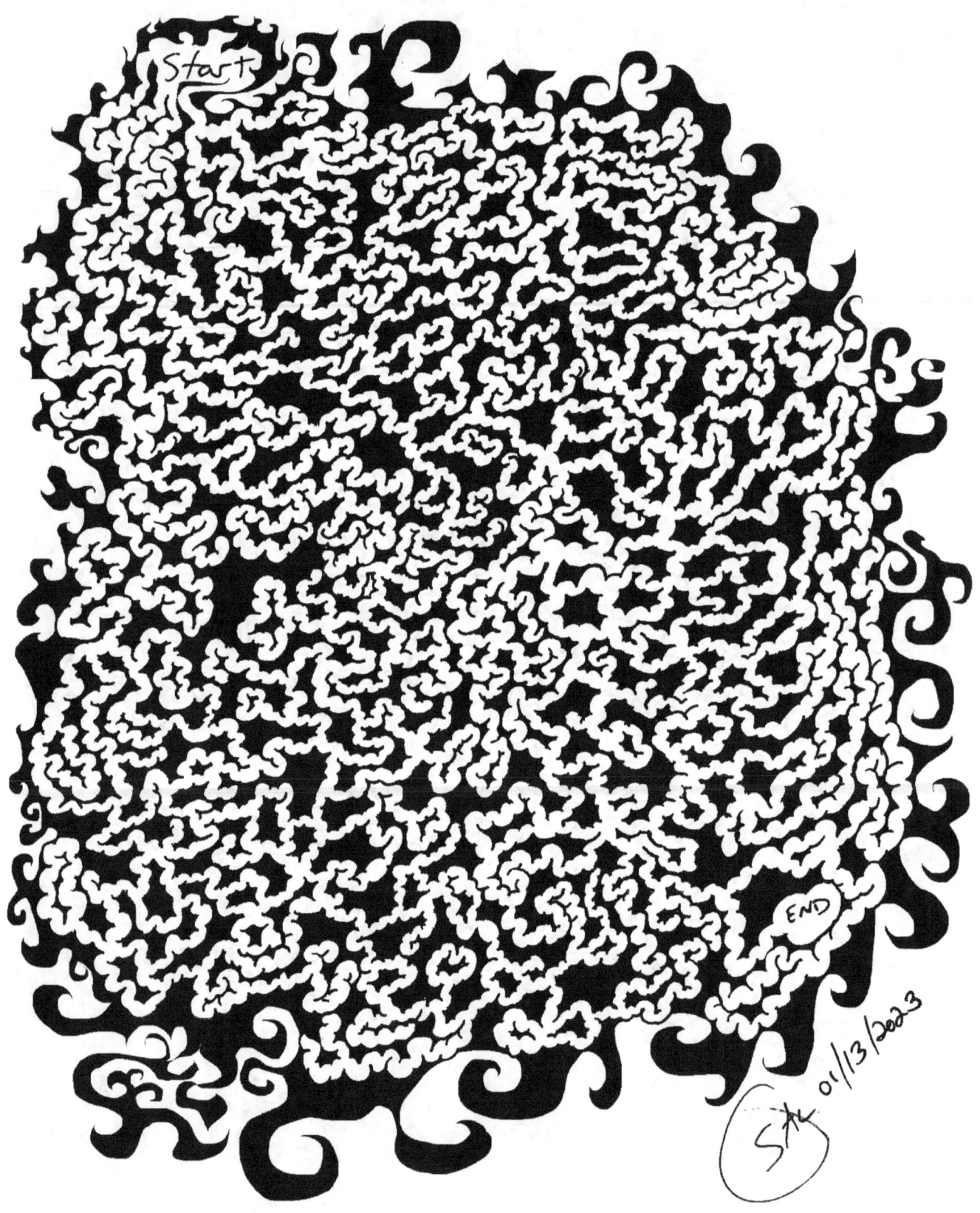

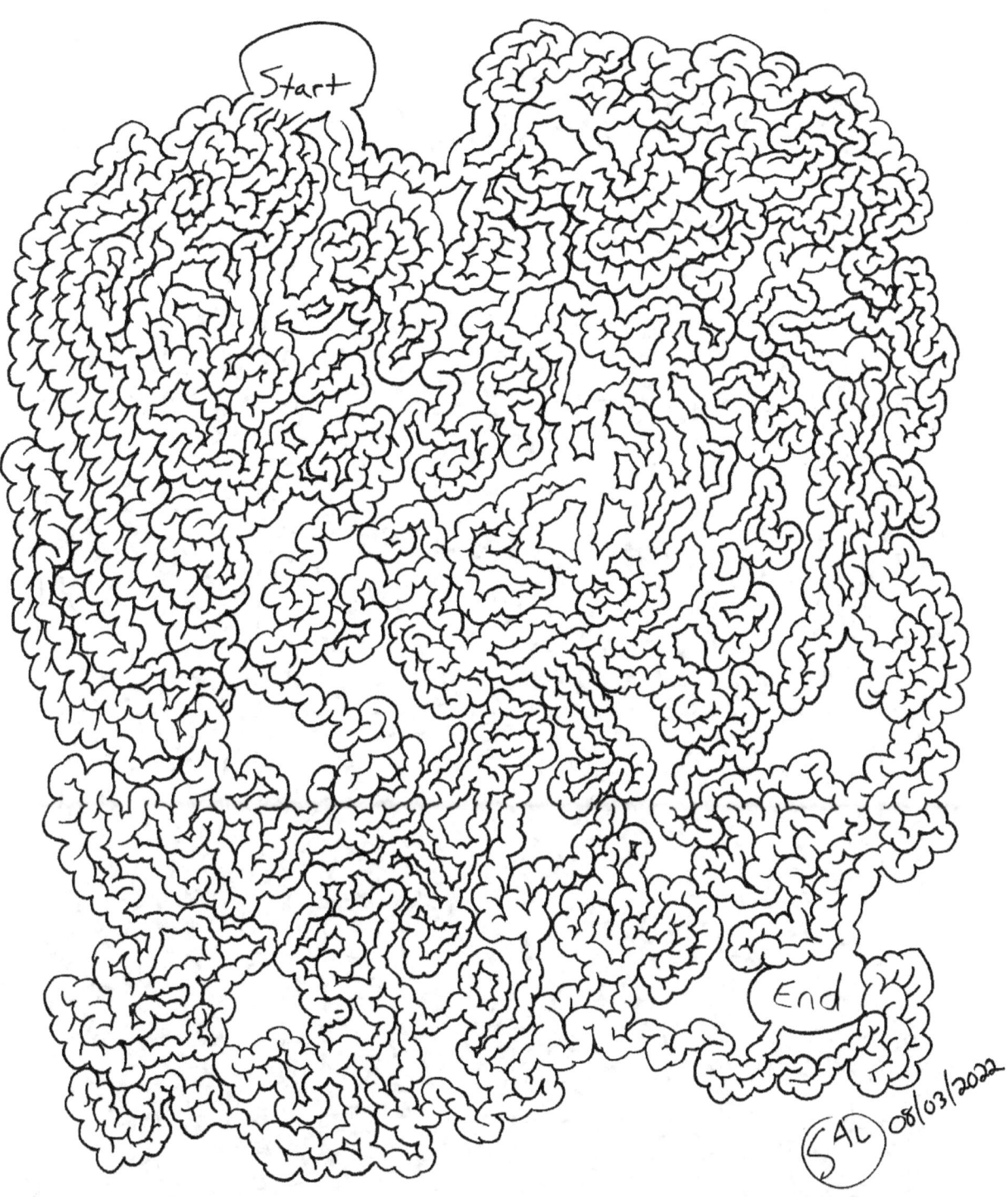

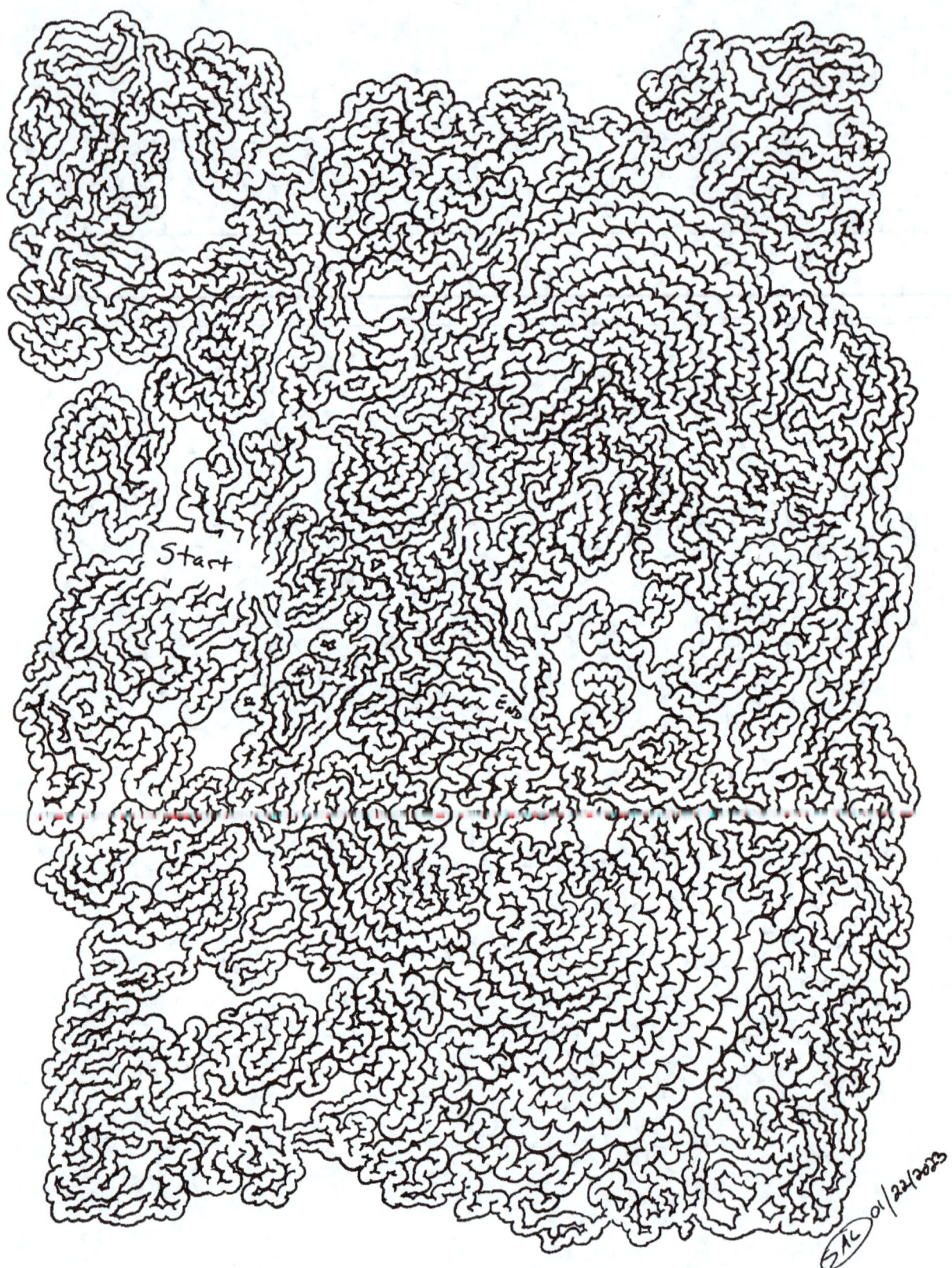

ABOUT THE ARTIST

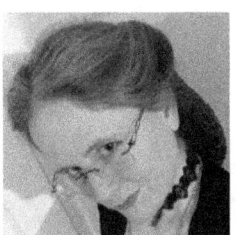

Stacie Ann Leininger

I am on multiple Spectrums including Autism and ADHD; in addition, I also have PTSD and Dyslexia. I have been writing and making mazes since childhood. I started giving away mazes in 5th grade and selling them at the behest of Andrea Walton (1980-2020). My first published literary piece appeared in a magazine when I was nine. In 2002, I earned a B.A. in English from the College of St. Rose where I was introduced to several members of the International Women's Writing Guild (IWWG).

In 2001, I self-published my first poetry chapbook titled *Sheep and a Blind Monkey* dedicated to Andrew James McMahon (Feb. 1980 – Dec. 1995). There have been several publications since then. Most recently: in 2019, I was published in *Dark Yonder: Tales & Tabs*, a crime anthology. In 2021, I released *Gleothane: A Call for Warriors* under my pseudonym Cora B. Edwin. *Gleothane* is an all-ages spin on the choose your own adventure, action, high fantasy comedy Andrew James McMahon and I started in November of 1995.

In 2022, I released *To Overcome is to Be: A Collection of Poems Written Between Ages 13 and 22* followed by *They Labeled Me Crazy: A Collection of Poems Written Between Ages 15 and 23*. These poetry books were compiled specifically for teenagers on the same invisible spectrums, I have, to help guide them in the writing world and assist their teachers by giving the teachers a basic poetry writer's guide for teenagers. These most recent works are available on Amazon.

While I continue to heal from a serious mental health crisis I am working on several more books. My works in progress include, but are not limited to the world of *Gleothane*, poetry books, a romantic comedy series, a crime comedy novella series, and mazes.

You can follow me on Instagram:
Stacie_Ann_Leininger
I also sell artwork merchandize on RedBubble.
Lastly, I'm on BookBub under the names Stacie Ann Leininger and Cora B. Edwin.